Problem Solving Handbook
A Step-by-Step Approach

Problem Solving Handbook
A Step-by-Step Approach

Rod Baxter

2016

Copyright © 2015 by Rod Baxter
Edited by Kelli Baxter

All rights reserved. This book or any portion thereof may not be reproduced or used in any manner whatsoever without the express written permission of the publisher, except for the use of brief quotations in a book review or scholarly journal.

First Edition: 2015
Second Edition: 2016

ISBN 9798359461009

Value Generation Partners, LLC
Naples, Florida 34109

You can follow the author at:
https://www.linkedin.com/in/rodbaxter/

With the purchase of this workbook, you are eligible to receive a complementary MS Excel® file, which contains the templates referenced in these chapters.

To download your complementary toolbox, please visit https://www.linkedin.com/company/value-generation-partners/ and select the Google Drive link.

Check out "Operational Excellence Handbook" by Rod Baxter for more problem-solving and process-improvement tools and techniques.

Contents

Introduction: Problem Solving for Success 1
    Background on A3 Thinking 5

Step One: State Problem and Goal 7
    Develop Problem Statement 7
    Define SMART Goal 9

Step Two: Understand Current Condition 11
    Document Current-State Process 11

Step Three: Conduct Root Cause Analysis 15
    Create a Cause-and-Effect (C&E) Diagram 15
    Conduct 5 Why Root Cause Analysis 17

Step Four: Construct Solutions 21
    Identify Potential Solutions 21
    Evaluate Solutions with Impact/Effort 23
    Pilot Test Solutions 25
    Document Future-State Process 26

Step Five: Execute Solutions 27

Step Six: Sustain Solutions 29
    A3 Sign-off and Solution Hand-Off 32

Step Seven: Salute the Team 33

Rapid Problem Solving for Success 35
    Rapid Problem-Solving Event 35
    Rapid Problem-Solving Workshop 36

Additional Problem-Solving Tools 39
    Affinity Diagram to Group Ideas 39
    Brainstorming to Generate Ideas 40
    Data Collection for Analysis 42
    Decision Tree for Selecting among Alternatives 45
    Fault Tree Analysis to Determine Root Cause 47
    FMEA to Understand Failure Modes and Effects 50
    Force Field Analysis to Understand Energies 53
    Graphical Analysis to Visualize Issues 55
    Meeting Agenda and Minutes 60
    Mind Mapping to Generate and Analyze Ideas 62
    Multivoting for Reaching Group Consensus 63

Contents

Nominal Group Technique to Generate/Rank Ideas.............. 65
Pairwise Comparison to Prioritize Options............................ 67
SIPOC to Summarize High-Level Process 69
Solution Selection Matrix for Prioritizing Ideas...................... 70
Status Reporting for Updating Stakeholders......................... 72
Training Plan for Sustaining Solutions 74

Summary: Problem Solving for Success 76

Introduction: Problem Solving for Success

Former Secretary of State, John Foster Dulles, is credited with the quote, "The measure of success is not whether you have a tough problem to deal with, but whether it is the same problem you had last year." Problems, also known as opportunities, issues, failures, defects, etc., come in many shapes and sizes and exist in every business and industry with varying levels of impact and complexity.

There are a variety of approaches, methodologies, and techniques to solve problems, including ISO Corrective Action, Ford 8D, A3 Thinking PDCA, Kepner-Tregoe®, Shainin®, and Lean Six Sigma DMAIC, to list a few. A simple, efficient, and effective approach to problem solving is one of the most lacking skills and sought-after competencies in business and industry today. Businesses need and want a simple approach to problem solving, one with predictable and sustainable solutions.

This simple seven-step, fact-based approach, called Problem Solving for Success, may be applied to any problem in any industry – healthcare, construction, manufacturing, service, hospitality, non-profit, government, financial, etc.

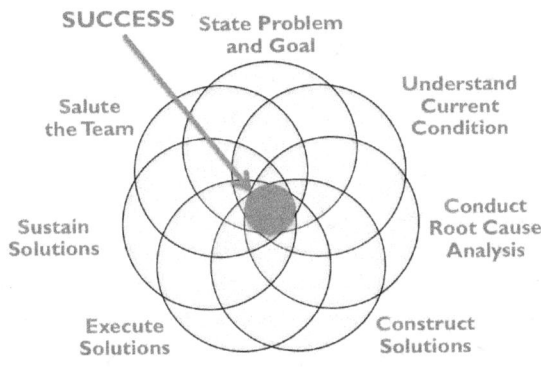

This guide to Problem Solving for Success is designed for problem solvers of all levels, regardless of their role, business, and industry. It combines the best elements of some of the simplest to most complex problem-solving approaches and methodologies into the following seven steps:

Introduction: Problem Solving for Success

1. **State Problem and Goal** – initiate the A3 Problem Solving for Success Worksheet, document the theme of the problem, define the problem, and create a SMART goal
2. **Understand Current Condition** – document the current-state process flow
3. **Conduct Root Cause Analysis** – create a cause-and-effect diagram, list issues with the current state, analyze data, and conduct 5 Why
4. **Construct Solutions** – list potential solutions, analyze for impact and effort, pilot test and verify solutions, and define the future-state process flow
5. **Execute Solutions** – define and execute a solution implementation plan
6. **Sustain Solutions** – define and execute a solution sustainment plan, conduct sign-off, and close the problem-solving effort
7. **Salute the Team** – recognize the team and celebrate success

Employing the seven-step process of Problem Solving for Success will result in a solution that solves the problem and sustains the results. The ensuing sections and chapters provide detail and information necessary to apply the seven-step Problem Solving for Success approach to every problem of any size and complexity for every industry and business.

Based on the complexity, time restrictions, resource availability, organizational goals and needs, etc., Problem Solving for Success may be conducted with one of two approaches. Problem solving may be conducted as a project-oriented approach as described in the seven-step Problem Solving for Success process sections of this handbook. Or, problem solving may be conducted in a condensed, event-based approach, as described in the Rapid Problem Solving for Success section.

The A3 Problem Solving for Success Worksheet, found in the *Problem Solving for Success Toolbox,* is used to guide problem-solving efforts. It is a variation of an A3 Thinking PDCA template, and it is used to document, summarize, and report problem-solving progress and status.

Introduction: Problem Solving for Success

A3 - Problem Solving for Success Worksheet

Theme:

Problem Solver: **Date:**

Problem Statement: no names, no solutions; list roles/functions, location, when, quantity, and cost:

SMART Goal: Specific – Measurable – Achievable – Relevant – Time-Bound:

Current State Process:

Cause and Effect Diagram or List of Issues with Current State:

Root Cause: why the problem occurred, was not detected, and was not prevented

Why 1:
Why 2:
Why 3:
Why 4:
Why 5:

Potential Solutions	Impact	Effort

Future State Process:

Actions to Implement the Solution	Who	When

Actions necessary to Sustain the Solution	Who	When

Sign-off **Date**

Introduction: Problem Solving for Success

A useful and powerful approach to support and supplement Problem Solving for Success is further defined in **Project Management for Success Handbook** and **Workshop Facilitation for Success Handbook**, and summarized in the following seven-step processes.

Project Management for Success Process:

Step One: Set-up the Project
Step Two: Understand the Requirements
Step Three: Create the Team
Step Four: Construct the Plan
Step Five: Execute the Plan
Step Six: Sign-off and Close the Project
Step Seven: Salute the Team

Workshop Facilitation for Success Process:

Step One: Set-up the Workshop Charter
Step Two: Understand the Logistics
Step Three: Create the Team
Step Four: Clarify the Roles and Responsibilities
Step Five: Execute the Workshop
Step Six: Share Status of Workshop
Step Seven: Salute the Team

Key to Problem Solving for Success is timely, concise, and appropriate communication. George Bernard Shaw was quoted as saying, "The single biggest problem in communication is the illusion that it has taken place." As you execute the seven-step problem-solving approach, you must ensure that in each step careful consideration is given to the impact on the many and various stakeholders and how that impact is communicated.

Benefits of timely and concise communication include:

- Facilitates securing support for the problem-solving effort
- Clarification of roles and responsibilities
- Status of the problem-solving effort
- Updates on issues, risks, and changes
- Updates on activities, implementation plans, and training plans

Introduction: Problem Solving for Success

We wish you much success in your pursuit of Problem Solving for Success, thereby generating greater organizational value!

Background on A3 Thinking

A3 originated with Toyota, due to efforts to get reporting to a concise, one-page, 11"x17" (A3 size) sheet of paper. These days, it includes much more and is known as A3 Thinking or Lean Thinking. Foundationally, A3 Thinking can be thought of as being supported by problem solving, mentoring and coaching, communication, and collaboration. There are seven key elements to A3 Thinking.

Seven Elements of A3 Thinking:

- **Logical Thinking Process** – using scientific method to get to the root cause
- **Objectivity** – use of facts and data to define the problem
- **Results and Process** – balancing between methodology and achieving results
- **Synthesis, Visualization, Distillation** – concise visual display of the information and data
- **Alignment** – having consensus of the problem causes and countermeasures
- **Coherency Within and Consistency Across** – results in a linkage to the root cause, countermeasures, company goals, and departmental/functional goals
- **Systems Viewpoint** – impact of countermeasures

The A3 Report resides on an 11"x17" sheet of paper; it may be used for various purposes, including problem solving, proposals, design efforts, and more. While the A3 report of the past has been a living document using paper and pencil, many A3 reports today take the form of an Excel or PowerPoint template. The keys are the A3 Thinking and the scientific method. By putting A3 Thinking together with the scientific method and the A3 Report, you now have a powerful problem-solving approach, which can be used at all levels of the organization to solve problems, and to report on the status and progress.

Introduction: Problem Solving for Success

The problem-solving methodology used in A3 Thinking is originally based on the continuous improvement cycle known as the Deming Cycle, or PDCA as depicted in the following storyboard image.

A3 Report Layout with PDCA	
Background - Why work on the Problem - When and Where did the Problem Start	**Future State and Countermeasures** - Depict the Future Process - Who, What, and When
Current State - Define the Problem - Depict the Current Process	
Goals and Objectives - What Constitutes Success - When will it be Completed	**Check Results and Impacts** - Measures and Metrics - Control Charts or Scorecard
Root Cause Analysis - Cause and Effect Diagram - 5 Why and Graphical Diagrams	**Follow-up** - Conduct Training - Adjust as Required

Benefits of A3 Thinking include:

- Consistent approach with common language
- Improved problem solving, decision making, and reduced risks
- Improved customer satisfaction with quality results
- Faster cycle times with less waste at a reduced cost
- Improved speed and sustainment of problem resolution
- Improved culture, employee engagement, and problem solving

Utilizing this consistent, powerful, and proven approach results in strengthening the capabilities of the workforce, accelerating the speed to resolution of problem solving, and the generation of valuable results.

Step One: State Problem and Goal

Step One of Problem Solving for Success is State Problem and Goal. In this step, the problem solver initiates an A3 Problem Solving for Success Worksheet by entering the theme of the problem, the problem statement, and a SMART goal representative of the problem. Techniques for developing the problem statement and defining a SMART goal are further discussed in the following two chapters. "A problem well defined is a problem half solved," said Henry Ford.

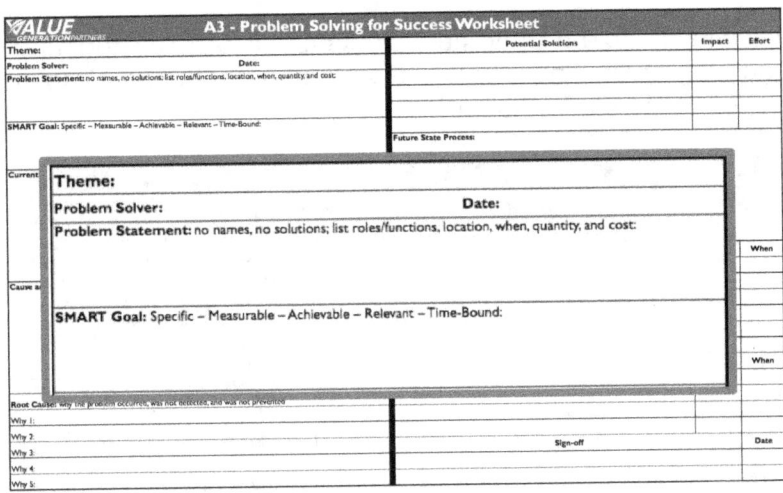

Develop Problem Statement

Developing a problem statement is critical to Problem Solving for Success. If the problem is not clearly defined and stated, a sustainable solution cannot be constructed and executed. Albert Einstein is often credited with the quote, "If I had an hour to solve a problem, I'd spend 55 minutes thinking about the problem and five minutes thinking about solutions." While the quote may be found in many forms, the basic premise is always the same: Invest time up front to ensure a successful outcome.

A well-written problem statement will generate understanding and support by others. It's a starting point for defining the situation

Step One: State Problem and Goal

relative to what the problem is, where it has occurred, when it occurred, and how severe it is.

Components of a problem definition and statement include:

- List roles or functions of individuals associated with the problem, without using names
- Describe specifically what the problem is, without listing solutions
- Describe when the problem occurred and when it was detected
- Describe where the problem is and is not located or detected
- List how many times and how often the problem occurred
- Quantify the costs associated with the problem

The following Problem Statement worksheet is a useful tool and approach for developing a problem statement for the A3 Problem Solving for Success Worksheet:

VALUE GENERATION PARTNERS	Problem Statement		
Problem Solver:		Date:	
Who:		List individuals associated with the problem without using names (Use roles or functions)	
What:		Describe specifically what the problem is without listing solutions	
When:		Describe when the problem occurred and when it was detected	
Where:		Describe where the problem is and is not located or detected	
How Often:		List how often the problem occurred	
How Many:		List how many times the problem occurred	
How Much:		Quantify the costs associated with the problem	
Problem Statement:			

What is wrong with these three problem statements, and how might they be better stated?

1. The emergency room patient wait time is too long
2. There are too many software coding errors
3. Our employee turnover rate is too high

Are the following three examples better problem definitions and statements?

Step One: State Problem and Goal

1. Hospital General North emergency room patient wait time is currently 90 minutes, which is three times the goal of 30 minutes; the extra wait time is resulting in patient safety concerns and satisfaction levels of 65%, as opposed to our goal of 97% satisfaction
2. Software by Us Corp. currently has a coding accuracy for point-of-sales devices in North America at an error rate of one error for every 10,000 lines of code, as opposed to the company goal of three coding errors per million lines of code; the current coding error rate is resulting in additional service and rework costs of $45,000 per one million lines of code
3. University of Learning's administrative turnover rate is currently 15% per year, as opposed to the university goal of 3% per year; the current turnover rate level costs the university $300K annually in hiring, onboarding, and training new administrative staff

Define SMART Goal

Defining a SMART goal is critical to Problem Solving for Success. Without a SMART goal, a sustainable solution cannot be constructed and executed.

The use of SMART goals has been credited to Peter Drucker, through his management by objectives concept. The first-known writing of the term "SMART" occurs in the November 1981 issue of Management Review, in George T. Doran's article, "There's a S.M.A.R.T. Way to Write Management's Goals and Objectives."

A discussion about problem solving would not be complete without talking about SMART goals. Consider the following three goals statements:

1. Shorten emergency room patient wait time
2. Improve software coding errors
3. Reduce our employee turnover rate

What is wrong with these three goals, and how might they be better stated? In each case, we don't know current quality levels, planned improvement levels, and when it will be complete. While these seem

Step One: State Problem and Goal

like admirable goals, it is not clear that the goals are in alignment with the strategies or within the scope of the problem-solving efforts.

How might we improve these three problem-solving goal statements using a SMART goal approach? A goal is considered **SMART** if it is **S**pecific, **M**easurable, **A**chievable, **R**elevant, and **T**ime-Bound.

The following SMART Goal worksheet is a useful tool and approach for defining a SMART goal for the A3 Problem Solving for Success Worksheet:

VALUE GENERATION PARTNERS	SMART Goal		
Problem Solver:		Date:	
Organization and location of goal			
Function and process of goal			
Current quality level of problem			
Desired quality level of goal			
Desired completion date of goal			
SMART Goal:			
Is the goal **Specific**?	Did you describe what process or outcome you plan to increase or decrease?		
Is the goal **Measurable**?	Did you list the current quality level and planned improvement level for when it is complete?		
Is the goal **Achievable**?	Did you base your planned quality level on facts and data?		
Is the goal **Relevant**?	Does your goal support the strategic initiatives of the organization and is it within your scope of influence and responsibility?		
Is the goal **Time-Bound**?	Did you list a date by which to achieve the improvement level?		

Do these three rewritten goals pass the SMART goal criteria?

1. Reduce Hospital General North Campus emergency room patient wait time from 90 minutes to the goal of 30 minutes by June 30 of this calendar year
2. Increase Software by Us coding accuracy for point-of-sales devices in North America from one error for every 10,000 lines of code to the company goal of three coding errors per million lines of code by December 31 of this calendar year
3. Reduce University of Learning's administrative turnover rate from the current 15% per year to the university goal of 3% per year by March 15 of this calendar year

If you cannot answer "yes" to all of the SMART goal questions in the template, continue to define the goal until you can.

Step Two: Understand Current Condition

Step Two of Problem Solving for Success is Understand Current Condition. W. Edwards Deming is credited with the phrase, "If you can't describe what you are doing as a process, you don't know what you're doing."

In this step, the problem solver documents the current-state process flow on the A3 Problem Solving for Success Worksheet. Various types of flow diagrams and process mapping techniques are further defined in the following chapter.

The chapters on SIPOC and data collection, in the section Additional Problem Solving Tools, may also be useful in understanding the current condition.

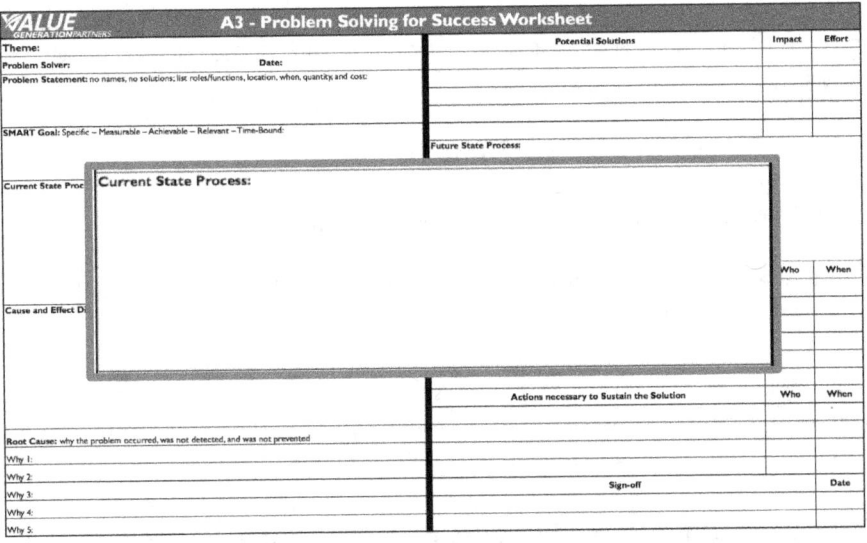

Document Current-State Process

Process flow diagrams are the tools used to visually describe the current state; it is what you are currently doing, how you are doing it, and provides input for problem solving and determining the root cause. These same process flow diagrams may be used later in the problem solving effort to define the future-state process flow and successfully implement and sustain solutions.

Step Two: Understand Current Condition

Process flow diagrams are made up of the following elements:

- **Inputs** that contribute to or influence a process step and output
- **Value-Added (VA)** process steps that transform the product or service in a way that adds value to the customer
- **Non-Value-Added (NVA)** process steps that do not transform the product or service in a way that adds value to the customer
- **Outputs** that result from a particular process step and inputs

All inputs have variation; all processes include value-added and non-value-added activities; and the outputs are the sum of the variation, value-added, and non-value-added activities. A well-defined and documented process flow diagram provides a starting point to understand the root cause, reduce variation, eliminate non-value-added activities, and solve problems.

Depending on the process, there are several types of process flow diagrams from which to choose to document the steps. Consider the following three examples.

1. Flowcharts and block diagrams
2. Input/output process map
3. Deployment flowcharts or swimlane maps

Below are some basic and typical symbols to use when creating flowcharts and process maps:

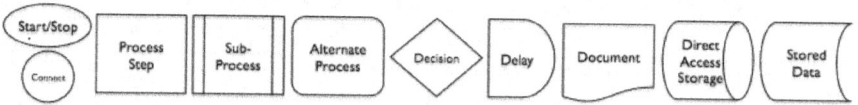

Flowcharts and block diagrams provide a high-level view of the process and are typically used to depict, analyze, and improve simple processes with few steps. Flowcharts may be used to document process flows that do not cross multiple functions or do not require an understanding of the inputs and outputs.

Step Two: Understand Current Condition

Flowchart or Block Diagram

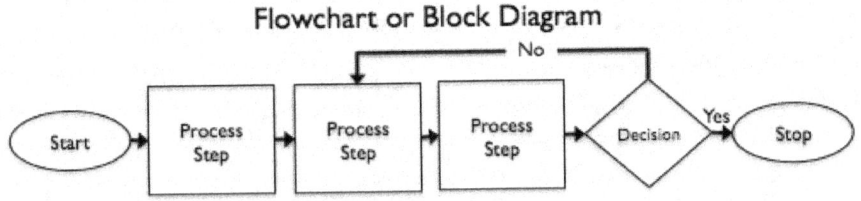

Input/output process maps are used to describe, understand, and improve processes with multiple steps that transform materials, services, or information into customer deliverables. These maps focus on understanding each process step, along with its associated inputs and outputs. Input/output process maps are typically used to find, understand, and correct sources of variation, determine control points, and to ensure the final output meets customer specifications.

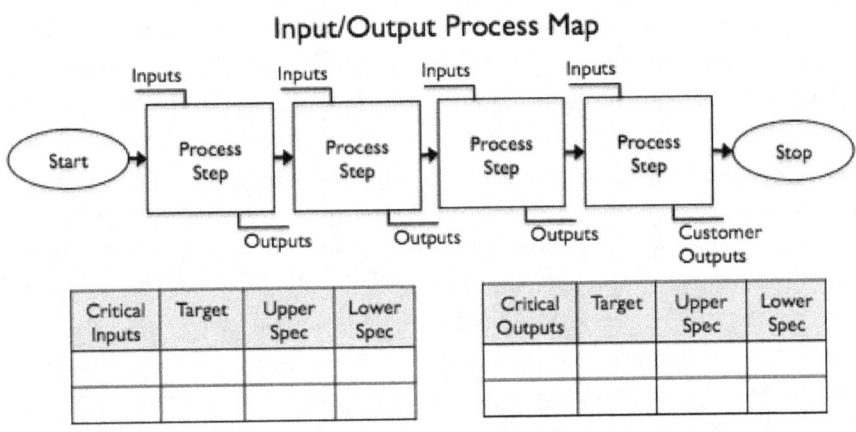

Deployment flowcharts or swimlane maps are used to understand and depict processes in situations when information, materials, and services flow with hand-offs across multiple functions. These maps are typically used to find, understand, and correct sources of non-value-added waste in transactional or business processes. While creating a deployment flowchart, it becomes clear where there are hand-offs, decision points, delays, loop backs, and redundant process steps.

Step Two: Understand Current Condition

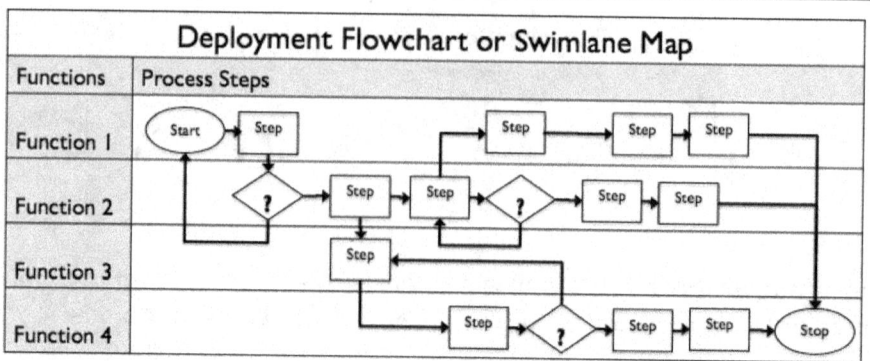

Step Three: Conduct Root Cause Analysis

Step Three of Problem Solving for Success is Conduct Root Cause Analysis. This step involves determining the true root cause of the problem statement developed in Step One: State Problem and Goal. Naoto Kan, former Prime Minister of Japan, is quoted as saying, "If you are unable to understand the cause of a problem, it is impossible to solve it."

In this step, the problem solver documents the cause and effect diagram and 5 Why root cause analysis on the A3 Problem Solving for Success Worksheet. Creating a cause-and-effect diagram and conducting 5 Why root cause analysis is further defined in the following two chapters.

The chapters on graphical analysis and fault tree analysis, in the section Additional Problem Solving Tools, may also be useful for understanding the true root cause of the problem.

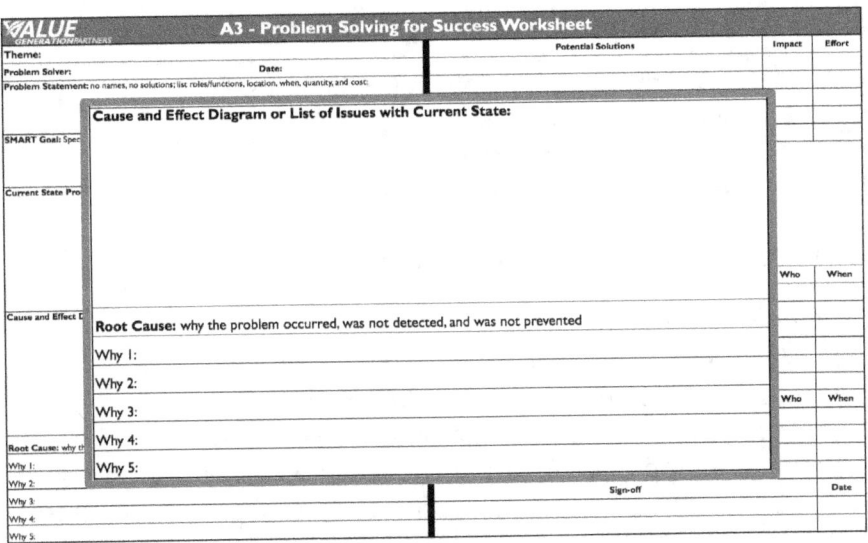

Create a Cause-and-Effect (C&E) Diagram

A simple yet powerful tool to use in a brainstorming session to quickly generate a list of many potential causes for an effect, problem, or outcome is the cause-and-effect diagram. It is also known as a

Step Three: Conduct Root Cause Analysis

fishbone diagram for its shape, as well as the Ishikawa diagram for its inventor Kaoru Ishikawa, who developed the technique in the late 1960s.

As defined in the following table, there are standard cause-and-effect diagram categories common to manufacturing, service, and marketing industries that may be used. Or, the categories may be derived based on the process, problem, or effect, which the diagram represents.

Manufacturing Industry	Service Industry	Marketing Industry
• Manpower • Mother Nature • Machines • Materials • Methods • Measurements	• Safety • Skills • Systems • Suppliers • Surroundings	• People • Price • Promotion • Place • Product • Process • Physical Evidence

When to use a cause-and-effect diagram:

- There are many varying opinions for the cause
- Team approach and team input are preferred
- Little or no quantitative data is available
- As a precursor to root-cause analysis

Benefits of a cause-and-effect diagram include:

- Place cause before solution
- Facilitate root cause analysis
- Provide a collaborative team environment
- Bring together diverse backgrounds and experiences
- Provide an approach to group causes into logical categories
- Save cost and time by determining and mitigating the true root cause

Cause-and-Effect Diagram Process:

1. Assemble a cross-functional team of subject matter experts who will be prepared for the cause-and-effect brainstorming session

Step Three: Conduct Root Cause Analysis

   with pre-work on the topic
2. Facilitate the session by stating and securing consensus for the problem or effect in the form of a "why" question (Example: Why are service calls taking six or more hours per call?)
3. Determine and secure consensus for the cause categories using the standard categories or others specific to the process related to the problem or effect
4. Draw the cause-and-effect diagram, listing the problem or effect and the categories for potential causes, as depicted in the following image
5. Brainstorm potential causes for each of the listed categories
6. Prioritize the most important potential causes for further analysis or use as input to additional tools, such as 5 Why root cause analysis or fault tree analysis

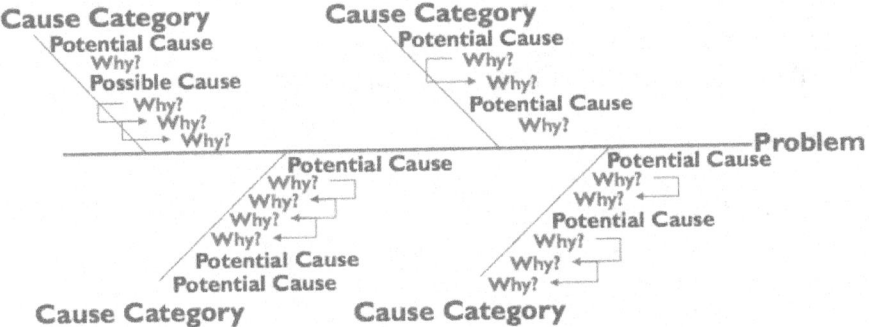

Conduct 5 Why Root Cause Analysis

Have you ever felt that you had solved a problem only to discover it is recurring? Likely the solution was applied to a symptom of the problem, rather than the actual root cause of the problem. Asking "why" five times is a great way to find the true root cause of a problem or defect, and lead to a solution, which will prevent recurrence. Sakichi Toyoda, the founder of Toyota Industries, developed the use of 5 Why in the 1930s as part of an evolving manufacturing process.

A farmer in a small Midwestern town once told me, "If you don't want weeds in your garden, you have to pull them out by the roots." I quickly learned how correct he was. You can't break off or kick a weed at ground level or even chop it off just below the ground's

Step Three: Conduct Root Cause Analysis

surface. The entire root must be removed or the weeds will come back, take over the garden, and choke out all of the valuable vegetables and plants. Removing the roots of the weeds is a lot of work, but the rewards are much greater than the sweat and labor.

The same can be said for solving problems. Invest the effort to understand and correct the true root cause of the problem, and the reward is a sustainable solution.

The 5 Why root cause analysis technique can be used as a stand-alone problem-solving tool, in combination with cause-and-effect analysis, or as an element of other tools and approaches.

Use 5 Why root cause analysis when:

- Root cause in not known
- Team approach and input are preferred
- Little or no quantitative data is available

Benefits of using 5 Why root cause analysis:

- Facilitate and identify root cause
- Determine root cause before solution
- Provide a collaborative team environment
- Bring together diverse backgrounds and experiences
- Save cost and time by determining and mitigating the root cause

5 Why Root Cause Process:

1. Assemble a cross-functional team of subject matter experts who will be prepared for the 5 Why root cause brainstorming session with pre-work
2. Facilitate the brainstorming session by securing consensus for the problem or defect definition, then document it on the following root cause analysis template

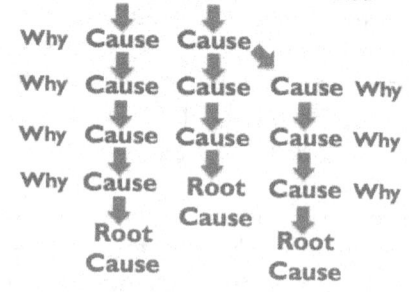

Step Three: Conduct Root Cause Analysis

3. Ask and write down why the problem or defect occurred, why it was not detected, and why it was not prevented, using the following 5 Why Root Cause Analysis template
4. Continue to ask "why" and write down responses until the root cause(s) is/are determined; the standard number of "why" questions is five, however it may take fewer or more to get to the true root cause; asking "why" may result in more than one answer, requiring branching to more than one root cause, as depicted in the root cause flow-down image

The following 5 Why worksheet is a useful tool and approach for determining the true root cause to apply to the A3 Problem Solving for Success Worksheet:

VALUE GENERATION PARTNERS — 5 Why Root-Cause Analysis

Problem Solver:		Date:	
Problem Statement:			
Why	Why did the Problem or Defect Occur?	Why was it not Detected?	Why was it not Prevented?
1st Why			
2nd Why			
3rd Why			
4th Why			
5th Why			

Step Four: Construct Solutions

Step Four of Problem Solving for Success is Construct Solutions. Tony Robbins is quoted as saying, "Identify your problems, but give your power and energy to solutions." This section describes the approach for identifying solutions and the process for selecting solutions that, when implemented, will eliminate the root cause and sustain results.

In this step, the problem solver documents solution selection and the future-state process on the A3 Problem Solving for Success Worksheet. Identifying and selecting solutions are further defined in the following four chapters.

Additional Problem Solving Tools section may also be useful for constructing solutions – specifically the chapters related to brainstorming, affinity diagram, mind mapping, solution selection, and decision tree.

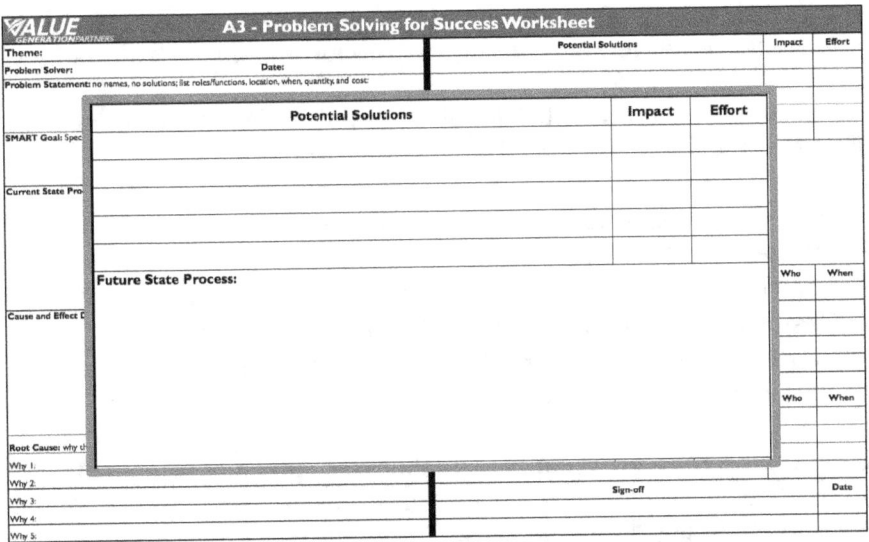

Identify Potential Solutions

Developing a list of potential solutions is the initial element of Step Four: Construct Solutions for Problem Solving for Success. Each root cause identified in Step Three: Conduct Root Cause Analysis will

Step Four: Construct Solutions

have a list of potential solutions from which to analyze and choose to carry forward to execution in Step Five: Execute Solutions.

There are several possible approaches to use to generate a list of potential solutions from which to choose, including:

- Benchmarking others in similar industries or with similar processes and approaches
- Looking to other departments or functions for best practices
- Using group decision tools such as brainstorming, affinity diagram, nominal group technique, and mind mapping
- Evaluating and analyzing the current-state process diagrams for opportunities

The following tools and techniques, as described in the section Additional Problem Solving Tools, are useful for developing lists of potential solutions:

- Brainstorming to generate ideas
- Affinity diagram to group/categorize ideas
- Mind mapping to generate and analyze ideas
- Nominal group technique to generate ideas and rank ideas

Prior to employing any of the following solution-evaluation and solution-selection techniques, remove any solutions that:

- Violate company norms, values, policies, and rules
- Violate laws or industry regulations
- Conflict directly with organizational strategies and directions
- Result in adverse effects to the business or customers
- Require significant non-budget capital or expense with no expected return on investment (ROI)

Based on the remaining list of potential solutions, the following tools, as described in the section Additional Problem Solving Tools, may be useful to make the final selection:

- Solution-selection matrix process
- Decision tree analysis

Step Four: Construct Solutions

During the evaluation and selection process, one should consider the following questions for each solution:

- What are the potential benefits?
- Are there technical, management, or resource risks?
- Are there risks to our business or our customers?
- Is the effort greater than the benefit?
- Are there organizational or cultural barriers?
- Does the solution correct and prevent the root cause?
- Are the costs to implement greater than the benefits?
- Does the solution add complexity beyond the current process?

It is truly important to understand the cause of the problem, and to keep the list of potential solutions as simple as possible.

"The story goes that when NASA first started sending astronauts into space, they soon learned that ballpoint pens would not work in zero gravity. To combat this problem, NASA scientists spent several years at significant costs to develop a pen that wrote in zero gravity, at any orientation, on nearly any surface, and at extreme cold and hot temperatures. The Russian astronauts simply used a pencil."

Evaluate Solutions with Impact/Effort

An impact/effort analysis is a powerful, yet simple, tool for prioritizing and choosing from many optional solutions. It is the process of using a matrix-style tool to evaluate several solutions against the impact gained and effort required for each option or idea. Impact/effort may be used in combination with other decision-making tools, such as solution-selection matrix and decision tree analysis.

Impact/effort analysis may be useful when:

- Quantitative, objective data is not available as part of the evaluation, selection, and decision-making process
- It is necessary to determine which potential solution is the best option for sustainable implementation
- A choice must be made from several options, and it is necessary to screen the options relative to impact gained and effort required

Benefits of impact/effort analysis include:

Step Four: Construct Solutions

- Provide a consistent and efficient approach for prioritizing and choosing from many optional solutions
- Reduce emotion and bias from the decision-making and prioritization process
- Provide a collaborative team environment
- Results of many options are displayed on one matrix-style tool

Impact/Effort Analysis Process:

1. Assemble a cross-functional team of subject matter experts (SMEs) who will be prepared for the session as a result of completing pre-work on the topic
2. Brainstorm a list of potential solutions for evaluation based on the impact/effort topic or use a prepared list from a previous brainstorming session
3. Construct an impact/effort matrix on a flipchart or use a template projected onto the screen
4. Evaluate each solution for impact gained and effort required, and place the option number or identification in the appropriate impact/effort cell on the matrix
5. Select and focus on the solutions with the highest impact at the lowest possible effort

The following Impact/Effort Matrix worksheet is a useful tool and approach for evaluating and prioritizing solutions for the A3 Problem Solving for Success Worksheet:

		Low	Medium	High
Impact/Benefit	High			
	Medium			
	Low			
		Effort/Cost		

VALUE GENERATION PARTNERS — Impact/Effort Matrix
Problem Solver: Date:

Step Four: Construct Solutions

An example of using an impact/effort matrix is by an improvement team working together to determine which of many solutions are best suited to reduce emergency room wait times. The team evaluates each solution for impact (how much it would reduce the emergency room wait time) and effort (how difficult and costly it will be to implement). Options with the highest impact and lowest effort are chosen to implement.

Impact/effort analysis is a powerful approach for prioritizing and choosing from multiple solution options.

While the matrix tool is described using impact and effort as evaluation categories, the same matrix – and approach – may be used to evaluate solutions against other categories, such as cost/benefit, impact/risk, value/effort, etc. The matrix indicates that the options are evaluated from a low, medium, and high perspective, yet the criteria may be replaced with elements based on specific and organizational needs. For example: Low, medium, and high may be replaced with appropriate dollar values, if the matrix would be used to do a cost/benefit analysis, rather than an impact/effort. As you can see, the matrix categories and criteria may be tailored to your organizational needs.

Pilot Test Solutions

A pilot test consists of testing a solution as if it is in the environment and process that it will eventually be implemented. This provides an opportunity to determine if the solution indeed eliminates the cause of the problem and results in no unintended consequences. It is advised to pilot test the solution on a small scale prior to spending time, resources, and money on a full-scale implementation.

Benefits of pilot testing the solution include:

- Mitigate potential risks of full-scale implementation
- Determine if the solution eliminates the root cause and prevents recurrence of the problem
- Determine the solution's effectiveness
- Determine that there are no negative impacts or unintended results from implementing the solution
- Understanding of any issues or problems associated with implementation of the solution

Step Four: Construct Solutions

- Test implementation plan, as well as the solution

When possible, use data, graphical analysis, and experimentation to verify the solution's effectiveness, as described in the section Additional Problem Solving Tools.

If the pilot test and graphical analysis fail to verify the solution's effectiveness to eliminate the root cause and prevent recurrence of the problem, return to the Solution Selection phase of Construct Solutions.

Document Future-State Process

Recall Step Two: Understand Current Condition. In that step, process flow diagrams are used to define current-state processes that include the root cause of a problem. The diagrams are then used as input to conduct root cause analysis.

In this step, the process flow diagrams are now used to define the future-state process, which no longer includes the root cause of the problem. You may use one of the following three process flow diagrams to update and document the future-state process – one that eliminates the root cause and prevents recurrence of the problem.

Flowcharts and block diagrams may be used to document process flows that do not cross multiple functions or do not require an understanding of the inputs and outputs.

Input/output process maps may be used to describe processes with multiple steps that transform materials, services, or information into customer deliverables and require an understanding of the inputs and outputs.

Deployment flowcharts or swimlane maps may be used to depict processes in situations when information, materials, and services flow with hand-offs across multiple functions.

Step Five: Execute Solutions

Step Five of Problem Solving for Success is Execute Solutions. As quoted by Tom Landry, "Setting a goal is not the main thing. It is deciding how you will go about achieving it and staying with that plan." The action plan to implement the solution is the tool to execute sustainable solutions.

In this step, the problem solver documents and executes actions to implement the solution. The chapters on meeting agenda, minutes, and status reporting, in the section Additional Problem Solving Tools, may also be useful for solution implementation.

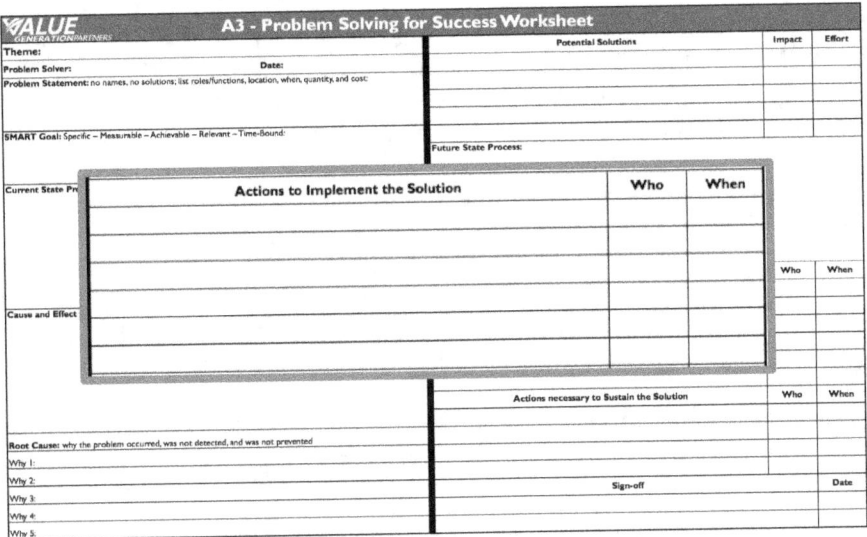

Process to Execute Solutions:

1. Define and document actions necessary to implement the solution; inputs to a solution implementation plan include details and results from the previous problem-solving step – Construct Solutions
2. Assign ownership of each action
3. Determine and document due dates for each action
4. Monitor the status of each action and implement countermeasures if an action due date is at risk, behind schedule, or not delivering the desired results

Step Five: Execute Solutions

5. Add actions to the implementation plan, as necessary

Benefits of an action plan to implement the solution include:

- Provide a collaborative team environment
- Save time and resources by managing solution implementation actions
- Increase focus and attention on solution implementation actions, due dates, and responsibilities
- Provide a consistent approach for efficiently and effectively managing solution implementation actions, due dates, and responsibilities
- Ensure implementation of sustainable solutions

Implementing solutions requires a degree of project management skill and discipline. A detailed solution implementation plan may be helpful and even necessary when solutions are complex and require extensive actions for successful implementation.

The following Solution Implementation Plan template is a useful supplement to the A3 Problem Solving for Success Worksheet:

VALUE GENERATION PARTNERS — Solution Implementation Plan

Problem Solver: Date:

#	Who / Owner	What / Task	When — Plan Date	Status	Other / Comments
1				Not Started	
2				On Schedule	
3				At Risk	
4				Behind	
5				Complete	
6				Cancelled	
7				Not Started	

Step Six: Sustain Solutions

Step Six of Problem Solving for Success is Sustain Solutions. Henry Ford is quoted as saying, "If you think you can or you think you can't, you're right." The solution sustainment plan is the tool to succeed with a sustainable solution.

In this step, the problem solver documents and executes actions necessary to sustain the solution. Sign-off on the A3 Problem Solving for Success Worksheet is secured upon verification of solution sustainment. The chapters on meeting agenda, minutes, status reporting, and training plan, in the section Additional Problem Solving Tools, may also be useful in solution sustainment.

Process to Sustain Solutions:

1. Define and document actions necessary to sustain the solution; inputs to a solution sustainment plan include details and results from the previous problem-solving steps – Conduct Root Cause Analysis, Construct Solutions, and Execute Solutions
2. Assign ownership of each action
3. Determine and document due dates for each action
4. Monitor the status each action and implement countermeasures, if an action is late or not delivering the desired results
5. Add actions to the sustainment plan, as necessary

Step Six: Sustain Solutions

6. Conduct training on the solution
7. Verify sustainment of the solution
8. Close and hand-off the solution

Benefits of an action plan to sustain the solution include:

- Increase focus on preventing recurrence of the root cause
- Provide a consistent approach for identifying and controlling critical process characteristics
- Provide an approach to ensure conformance to specifications and customer requirements
- Save time and resources by controlling critical process characteristics

A solution sustainment plan is essentially a summary of the types of controls that will be used to monitor and sustain critical characteristics of the solution. It is a method for assuring that improvements will be sustained once changes have been implemented.

Regardless of the approach used for problem solving, a sustainment plan is a critical component to any problem-solving effort. Defining and deploying a comprehensive sustainment plan takes careful thought and consideration by the team to ensure critical control elements are included.

A sustainment plan can be a stand-alone document for ongoing control long after the problem-solving effort is completed. Such a plan should be reviewed periodically and updated as necessary by the process owner to ensure it is current and effective.

A solution sustainment plan is used when:

- The solution results in changes to the process, product, or service
- The solution results in changes in roles and responsibilities
- A solution includes critical characteristics
- Products or services move across changes in ownership

Common types of solution sustainment include:

- Layered audits, process audits, and internal audits

Step Six: Sustain Solutions

- Help chains
- Automated controls
- In-process inspections
- Statistical Process Control (SPC)
- Total Preventive Maintenance (TPM)
- Updated flow diagrams, work instructions, procedures, etc.
- Training is updated and delivered

Considerations when creating a solution sustainment plan include:

- What input variables are critical to process performance?
- What process characteristics will be monitored?
- At what point in the process is it best to monitor key inputs?
- What are the specifications of the control characteristics?
- What type of control method will be used?
- How often is the characteristic measured and what sample size?
- How will the characteristic be measured?
- Who will be responsible for monitoring the characteristic?
- What is the signal to indicate an out-of-control condition?
- What is the corrective action for an out-of-control condition?
- Who is responsible for the corrective action?

Solution Sustainment Plan Process:

1. Define sustainment characteristics, method, and frequency
2. Determine and assign ownership of the solution sustainment characteristics; ownership and responsibility should be assigned to a person or group who will own the sustainment long after the problem-solving effort is closed
3. Define out-of-control signal and corrective action
4. Determine and assign person or group responsible for corrective action; ownership and responsibility should be assigned to a person or group who will own the corrective action long after the problem-solving effort is closed

The following template is a useful supplement to the A3 Problem Solving for Success Worksheet when detailed and ongoing sustainment actions are necessary:

Step Six: Sustain Solutions

VALUE GENERATION PARTNERS — Solution Sustainment Plan

Problem Solver:							Date:	
Who / Owner	What / Sustainment Characteristic	When / Sustainment Frequency/Timing	How / Sustainment Method	What / Signal	Who / Responsible	How / Corrective Action	Other / Comments	

A3 Sign-off and Solution Hand-Off

An exciting and rewarding time in a problem-solving effort is A3 sign-off and solution hand-off. It's when you validate that all of the *t*'s have been crossed and *i*'s have been dotted.

A3 Sign-off and Solution Hand-off Process:

1. Validate that the SMART goal has been achieved and an effective solution sustainment plan is deployed
2. Validate that processes, procedures, records, and training are updated and delivered
3. Confirm that products, processes, or services are delivered to the customer or process owner
4. Secure acceptance of the products, processes, or services from the customer and/or process owner
5. Conduct final review, document lessons learned, and archive problem-solving documents and artifacts
6. Deliver final A3 Problem Solving for Success report-out and secure sign-off on the A3

Benefits of problem-solving A3 sign-off and solution hand-off include:

- Provide a collaborative, motivational team environment
- Provide a smooth transition of ownership of deliverables
- Provide a consistent approach for efficiently and effectively completing problem-solving efforts
- Result in a customer-centric approach and environment

Step Seven: Salute the Team

Step Seven of Problem Solving for Success is Salute the Team. Key elements of this final step include 1) celebrating success of solving the problem and 2) sustaining the solution, as well as 3) recognition of team members and their contributions.

Henry Ford, the founder of Ford Motor Company, delivered a clear and concise message regarding the importance of teams and the power of team building by saying, "Coming together is a beginning. Keeping together is progress. Working together is success." The strength and success of an organization's problem-solving efforts are highly dependent on a strong team culture.

Team recognition and celebration are critical to the success of future problem-solving efforts and to enhance organizational culture. Recognition and celebration should provide positive reinforcement, in a setting instrumental to personal reward, and should be conducted or attended by leadership and senior management.

Saluting the team should be carried out in a public forum, providing team members with recognition from leadership and motivation from peers. This step in Problem Solving for Success ensures that team members will support the next problem-solving effort and others will be motivated to join future problem-solving efforts.

Methods and approaches to saluting the team include:

- Monthly newsletter
- Website, intranet, social media
- Special celebration and recognition meeting
- Company gifts (logo hats, shirts, mugs, etc.)
- Gift certificates
- Team, staff, and leadership meetings

Benefits of saluting the team include:

- Provide sense of purpose
- Communicate business results
- Reinforce positive outcomes
- Collaborative environment

Step Seven: Salute the Team

- Sense of belonging
- Skill development and learning
- Silos and barriers do not exist
- Efficiently and effectively resolve issues that individuals alone cannot resolve
- Inclusive environment in which teams work toward common goals

Congratulations on completing your Problem Solving for Success efforts! We wish you continued success in your pursuit of solving problems and sustaining solutions, thereby generating greater organizational value!

Rapid Problem Solving for Success

Rapid problem solving is an effective and efficient approach to solving problems and executing sustainable solutions in a rapid and condensed manner. Rapid problem solving may be conducted for many purposes, such as customer issues, error reduction, defect reduction, cycle time reduction, process improvement, waste reduction, cost-of-quality reduction, etc. Rapid problem solving may be conducted in the form of an event or a workshop, depending on the problem complexity, urgency, and span of impact.

Regardless of the approach – event or workshop – an A3 Problem Solving for Success Worksheet is utilized to guide and document the problem-solving effort.

Rapid Problem-Solving Event

A rapid problem-solving event is the quickest approach to problem solving. Rapid problem-solving events typically require less than a few hours to complete and are conducted in quick response to urgent and critical issues. The problem solver in a rapid problem-solving event is typically the owner of the problem or process in which the problem has occurred.

Rapid problem-solving events are methodical approaches to quickly solve problems and implement sustainable solutions. It is not a "fire fighting" approach to applying a "Band-Aid" fix to the symptom of a problem. Rapid problem solving requires a thorough understanding of the problem, determination of the root cause, and implementation of a sustainable solution to prevent recurrence of the problem.

Rapid problem-solving events may be useful when:

- Problem is isolated to a single piece of equipment or process
- A line is shut down and operations must resume quickly
- Customer delivery requirements are at risk or have been missed
- Safety accident or near miss has occurred
- Regulation or legal compliance is at risk
- Problem solving must be done quickly; time is of the essence

Benefits of rapid problem-solving events include:

Rapid Problem Solving for Success

- Sustainable solutions implemented quickly
- Provide a collaborative environment
- Provide a consistent and fact-based approach
- Increase focus and attention on solving problems
- Save time and resources through rapid solution execution

Rapid Problem-Solving Event Process:

1. An urgent and critical need for problem solving is identified
2. Problem solver determined that problem solving can and must be conducted as a rapid event
3. Problem solver quickly brings together the appropriate participants and subject matter experts necessary to solve the problem, preferably at the physical location of the problem
4. Problem solver facilitates participants through rapid problem solving using the A3 Problem Solving for Success Worksheet - define problem and goal, document current process, identify cause of problem, conduct 5 Why root cause analysis, determine solutions to eliminate cause, define future-state process, implement sustainable solutions, sign-off and celebrate success
5. The rapid problem-solving team dis-bans and goes about their normal daily work

Rapid Problem-Solving Workshop

A rapid problem-solving workshop brings together subject matter experts and process owners in a facilitated session to solve problems and implement sustainable solutions. Rapid problem-solving workshops are typically conducted in one to three days, and may result in a 30-day action plan that will be used for implementing and sustaining solutions.

The rapid problem-solving workshop facilitator may or may not be the problem/process owner. Much thought and consideration must be given to planning and conducting rapid problem-solving workshops in order to ensure a successful outcome.

Rapid problem-solving workshops may be useful when:

- Quality levels are deteriorating and solutions are not readily available

Rapid Problem Solving for Success

- There are many, varying opinions about how to solve a problem
- Problem solving must be done quickly; time is of the essence
- A customer is not receiving products or services as intended
- Team and cross-functional collaboration are necessary
- It is necessary for a group to work in a face-to-face environment
- Goals include waste reduction, cycle-time reduction, process improvement, cost reduction, or quality improvement

Benefits of rapid problem-solving workshops include:

- Provide a collaborative team environment
- Provide a consistent approach for facilitating workshops
- Increase focus and attention on customer satisfaction
- Save time and resources through rapid solution execution
- Increase focus and attention on continuous improvement efforts
- Provide an approach to efficiently and effectively solve problems

Rapid Problem-Solving Workshop Process:

Pre-Workshop

1. Sponsor determines need for problem-solving workshop
2. Sponsor identifies problem-solving facilitator
3. Facilitator and sponsor develop problem statement and SMART goal on an A3 Problem Solving for Success Worksheet
4. Facilitator and sponsor determine date, duration, location
5. Facilitator and sponsor identify participants
6. Sponsor notifies participants of the purpose, deliverables, roles, and responsibilities
7. Facilitator provides participants with pre-work
8. Facilitator secures location and supplies, such as flip charts, Post-it® notes, markers, tape, digital projector, etc.

Rapid Problem-Solving Workshop

9. Facilitator arrives in advance to ensure set-up and preparation, such as U-shape room arrangement, refreshments (beverages and snacks), workshop supplies, etc.
10. Facilitator and sponsor kick-off workshop - review agenda, deliverables, and scope; conduct introductions; establish ground rules; describe roles, responsibilities, and logistics

Rapid Problem Solving for Success

11. Step One: State Problem and Goal – participants review, refine, and approve problem statement and SMART goal
12. Step Two: Understand Current Condition – participants document current-state process flow
13. Step Three: Conduct Root Cause Analysis – participants create a cause and effect diagram, list issues with the current state, and conduct 5 Why analysis to determine the root cause of the issues and problem
14. Step Four: Construct Solutions – participants list potential solutions, analyze for impact and effort, pilot test and verify solutions, and define future-state process flow
15. Step Five: Execute Solutions – ideally the solution is executed as part of the rapid problem-solving workshop; however, if not possible due to time, technology, etc., participants define actions to implement the solution post-workshop
16. Step Six: Sustain Solutions – ideally solution sustainment is completed as part of the rapid problem-solving workshop; however, if not possible due to time, technology, etc., participants define actions necessary to sustain the solution post-workshop
17. Step Seven: Salute the Team – participants conduct workshop report-out with the sponsor and key stakeholders; participants, not the facilitator, present the report-out; secure approval to proceed with the implementation and sustainment plan; congratulate and release team members

Post-Workshop

18. If not done during workshop, loop back to Steps Five and Six: Execute Solutions and Sustain Solutions – facilitate actions to implement and sustain solutions; update sponsor based on the implementation and sustainment status; conduct sign-off and solution hand-off with the sponsor and process owner
19. If not done during workshop, loop back to Step Seven: Salute the Team – A3 owner and sponsor conduct celebration (virtual or in person) with team

Congratulations on completing Rapid Problem Solving for Success! We wish you continued success in your pursuit of solving problems and sustaining solutions, thereby generating greater organizational value!

Additional Problem-Solving Tools

The following problem solving tools and techniques may be used in support of or as alternatives to those described in the seven-step Problem Solving for Success process.

Affinity Diagram to Group Ideas

Affinity diagram – also known as KJ Method, for Kawakita Jiro, who developed the technique in the 1960s – is a simple and powerful tool for grouping many ideas and data into natural themes.

Affinity diagrams may be used to:

- Group and understand existing data, such as voice of the customer, surveys and interviews, and warranty and call logs
- Group and understand new data, such as brainstorming ideas on a specific topic
- Facilitate creative thinking
- Facilitate consensus

Creating an affinity diagram for new data requires facilitation skills and an understanding of brainstorming techniques.

Benefits of creating an affinity diagram include:

- Provide an approach to identify and group similar ideas into logical themes
- Provide a collaborative team environment
- Bring together diverse backgrounds and experiences

Affinity Diagram Process:

1. Assemble a cross-functional team of subject matter experts who were briefed and come prepared to thoughtfully engage in the affinity session topic
2. Silently jot down on a Post-it® note or 3x5 index card – using a verb and a noun – one idea or phrase

Additional Problem-Solving Tools

3. Randomly post the ideas on a board or wall, with no discussion or evaluation
4. Silently read, sort, and group the ideas into common themes; it may be necessary to limit the number of ideas per theme group; participants may wish to sort and group themed ideas into sub-themes
5. Define and name the themes based on the content of the ideas
6. Prioritize or vote for most important themes for further work or analysis; themes may be used for design or problem-solving efforts; also, themes may be used as input to additional tools, such as a data collection plan or cause-and-effect diagram

An example of using affinity diagram is typified by a team tasked with reducing infection rates in a hospital operating room. The team brainstorms nearly 70 potential ideas intended to reduce infection rates. An affinity diagram is used to group the ideas into six major themes. Then, those six themes are further evaluated and defined for implementation.

Brainstorming to Generate Ideas

Brainstorming is likely the single most beneficial tool for generating powerful and useful ideas in a group or team environment. It is an efficient and effective method for generating ideas within a team by allowing participants to be creative, unbound by current paradigms. Alex F. Osborn, known as the father of brainstorming, is quoted as saying, "It is easier to tone down a wild idea than to think up a new one."

Brainstorming ground rules:

- No idea is a bad idea
- Encourage participation from all group members
- Do not evaluate, criticize, or judge ideas

Additional Problem-Solving Tools

- Solicit quantity of ideas
- No titles in the room, meaning every idea carries same value
- Record ideas; build on those ideas

Brainstorming may be used when:

- There is a desire to generate many ideas
- Team approach and input are preferred
- Little or no quantitative data is available
- Creative thinking and problem solving are useful

Benefits of brainstorming include:

- Provide a collaborative team environment
- Provide a consistent approach for generating ideas
- Bring together diverse backgrounds and experiences
- Provide an approach for fun, creative thinking, and new ideas
- Provide an effective and efficient approach for generating ideas

Brainstorming Process:

1. Assemble a cross-functional team of participants who are briefed and come prepared to engage in the brainstorming session
2. Open session and prepare participants by facilitating introductions and reviewing the brainstorming topic, ground rules, expectations, concerns, and deliverables of the session
3. Allow participants a few minutes in silence to think about ideas related to the brainstorming topic and session deliverables; participants will have been briefed and prepared for the topic prior to conducting the session
4. In a free-flow setting, ask participants to share their ideas with no discussion or evaluation
5. The facilitator records each idea exactly as presented on a flip chart
6. Continue presenting and recording ideas until participants have no other ideas to add to the list, or the agreed-upon time limit is reached

Use the brainstorming ideas for the next phase, such as affinity diagram, implementation plan, impact/effort matrix, multivoting, solution selection matrix, etc.

Additional Problem-Solving Tools

Data Collection for Analysis

Creating a comprehensive data collection plan takes careful thought and consideration by the team to ensure time and expenses are not wasted on unnecessary data collection. Sir Josiah Stamp is credited with the quote, "Public agencies are very keen on amassing statistics – they collect them, raise them to the nth power, take the cube root, and prepare wonderful diagrams. But what you must remember is that every one of the numbers comes in the first instance from the village watchman, who just puts down what he darn well pleases."

There are three data collection strategies to consider; these will help guide development of a data collection plan.

1. **Retrospective (Historical)** data collection is a passive strategy using data from records, systems, and files. It is typically the most accessible and the least expensive to collect. You must always be cautious using this data collection strategy, however, because you may not know how the data was originally collected or who collected it. And it may not truly represent the current process being analyzed.
2. **Observational** data collection is a passive strategy in which you or a team member collect(s) data while observing the process in its current state. This data collection strategy will typically result in more time and greater cost than retrospective data collection. However, it may better represent the true process in its current state. This strategy will also be necessary, if the data required has not been documented or collected in the past.
3. **Experimental** data collection is an active strategy used to find cause-and-effect relationships. This strategy provides the team with information to optimize the process output by fine-tuning process inputs.

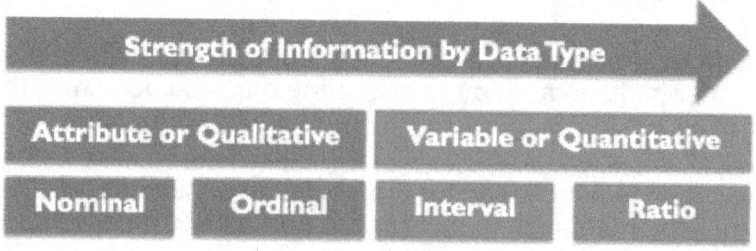

The four main types of data to consider for the data collection plan are nominal, ordinal, interval, and ratio. Nominal and ordinal are the least informative of the four data types. It is important to consider what questions need answered with the data analysis, which will determine what data types need collected.

1. **Nominal** (attribute or qualitative) data is defined as categories or names of information, such as colors, locations, brands, products, etc.
2. **Ordinal** (attribute or qualitative) data is non-numeric ordered categories, such as 1st, 2nd, 3rd, or strongly agree, agree, neutral, disagree, strongly disagree. While it is clear that there is an order to categories, what is not clear is the relative difference between each category.
3. **Interval** (quantitative) data is numeric data arranged in order with meaningful and exact differences – like temperature, for example. Interval data is more informative than attribute data types – because we can add or subtract temperature readings and we can calculate statistics, such as mean and standard deviation – but we cannot multiply, divide, or calculate ratios, because there is no true zero (i.e.: it is not possible to have no temperature).
4. **Ratio** (quantitative) data is the most informative of the data types. It has all of the same characteristics of interval data, plus it has a defined zero and supports many more statistical models and analyses.

Data collection requires selecting samples that are appropriate to estimate the characteristics of the population. Considerations for defining sample plans are that the data must be representative of the population, mitigate variation, and take into account all cost implications. Types of sampling plans include:

- **Simple random sampling** - calculated number of random samples from a batch or group
- **Stratified random sampling** - calculated number of random samples per stratification group
- **Systematic random sampling** - taking every *nth* sample from a group
- **Subgroup sampling** - taking a planned number of consecutive samples during each defined time period

Additional Problem-Solving Tools

Some considerations when creating a data collection plan include:

- What questions do we want to answer through data analysis?
- What are the process input variables?
- What inputs will we use to design data collection forms?
- What are the various cycles of the process?
- How can we achieve a representative sample?
- Who will collect the data?
- Are we using accurate operational definitions?
- What issues or barriers might we encounter?

A data collection plan is used when:

- Data is not readily available for analysis
- Root cause is not known and an analytical review is necessary
- Quantitative analysis is necessary as part of the root cause analysis process

Benefits of a data collection plan include:

- Provide a consistent approach for identifying, documenting, and communicating data collection needs
- Lead to efficient and effective data collection and analysis
- Save time and cost by prioritizing data collection needs
- Create a collaborative team culture

Data Collection Plan Process:

1. Assemble a cross-functional team of subject matter experts who will be prepared for the data collection plan development session with pre-work on the topic
2. Review inputs to the data collection plan such as process maps and cause-and-effect diagram
3. Determine the questions to be answered with data collection and analysis
4. Determine the operational definition of data, data type, sample size or frequency, and responsibility
5. Determine date and time, recording method, and measurement method
6. Initiate data collection; revise the plan based on analysis and learnings

Additional Problem-Solving Tools

The following template works well for creating and managing a data collection plan as part of a problem solving effort:

VALUE GENERATION PARTNERS			Data Collection Plan				Date:	
Problem Solver:								
Who	What			When		Why	How	Other
Responsible	Operational Definition	Data Type	Sample size or Frequency	Date and Time	Questions to be Answered		Recording Method	Collection Method (Gage)	Comments

Decision Tree for Selecting among Alternatives

A decision tree is a useful tool for defining, analyzing, and choosing between several alternative solutions by understanding the outcomes for each. It is a tree diagram visually displaying alternative decisions, including probability, expected value, and outcome for each. Decision tree analysis may be used in combination with other decision-making tools, such as solution selection matrix and impact/effort matrix.

A decision tree may be useful when:

- Little quantitative data is available
- Opinions vary on the best solution
- It is necessary to make a decision from among several alternative solutions
- The decision may result in considerable expense and potential risks

Benefits of a decision tree include:

- Fun; easy to use and understand
- Can be conducted alone or with a team; if facilitated with a team, it will bring together diverse backgrounds and experiences and provide a collaborative team environment
- Support decision making when little data is available
- Provide input to additional decision-making approaches
- Ability to build in new scenarios and outcomes

Additional Problem-Solving Tools

- Provide an approach to analyze, challenge, and prioritize alternative solutions
- Provide an approach to determine probability, expected values, and consequences of alternative decisions

Common decision tree symbols include:

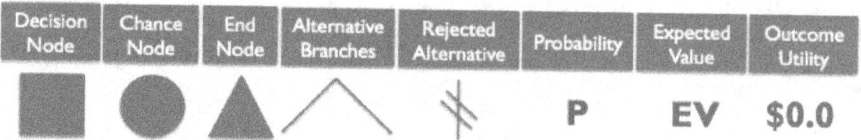

The following image is an example of a decision tree diagram with "Software Solution" as the subject of the decision.

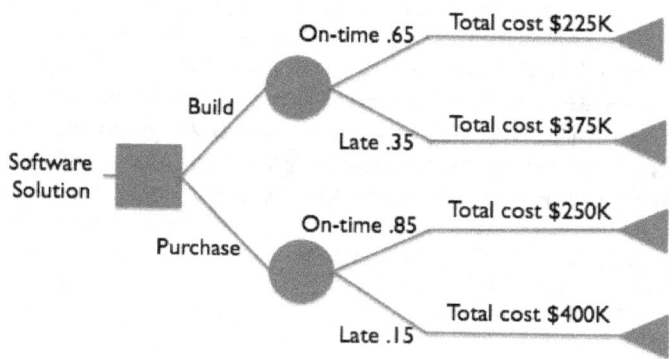

Decision Tree Process:

1. Define the subject for which you must make a decision; inputs to a decision tree may include SMART goal setting, solution selection, and constructing a solution
2. Document the subject of the decision tree on paper or flip chart, or in an electronic format
3. Add potential decisions to the decision tree subject
4. Add probability and outcome for each decision
5. Validate that all decision choices, probabilities, and outcomes have been considered and are added to the decision tree
6. Analyze the decision tree to determine the best decision choice using probabilities, outcomes, and expected values to support the final decision

Fault Tree Analysis to Determine Root Cause

Fault tree analysis is an effective tool for root cause analysis, followed by implementation of solutions to correct the cause. Originally developed in the early 1960s, fault tree analysis (FTA) was used to conduct top-down failure analysis. Primarily used in safety and reliability engineering for preventive analysis to reduce risk and prevent failure, FTA is now used in a wide range of industries and scenarios. FTA may be used in combination with other root cause analysis tools, such as cause-and-effect matrix and 5 Why root cause analysis.

FTA starts with a single top-level event or failure, which is analyzed to determine actual input faults and their root causes. A solution implementation plan to eliminate causes of input faults (root causes) to the top-level failure is determined and launched as a result of the fault tree analysis.

The following image depicts a basic fault tree diagram example.

Fault tree top-level, input/fault, and gate example

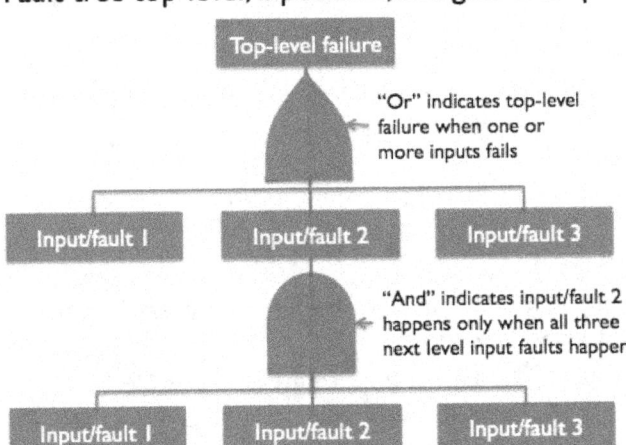

A fault tree analysis may be useful when:

- Quantitative data may be limited
- Opinions vary on the relationships between inputs and the top-level failure

Additional Problem-Solving Tools

- It is desirable to understand and correct causes of the top-level failure
- It is necessary and important to prioritize inputs that could lead to the top-level failure

Benefits of a fault tree analysis include:

- May be conducted alone or as a team; if conducted as a team, it will bring together diverse backgrounds and experiences
- Facilitate root-cause analysis
- Provide an approach to analyze and prioritize inputs or faults
- Identify and eliminate causes of the top-level failure

Common fault tree symbols include:

- Basic Event – Failure event in a process, system, or component requiring no additional analysis
- External Event – An event that is normally expected to occur
- Undeveloped Event – An event where information is not available or is determined to be unimportant
- Conditioning Event – A condition or restriction applied to a logic gate
- Intermediate Event – Used to include additional event information
- Transfer In/Out – Used to indicate a transfer to a related fault tree
- Or Gate – The event occurs if one or more of the input events occur
- And Gate – The event occurs if all of the input events occur
- Exclusive Or Gate – The event occurs if one and only one input event occurs
- Priority And Gate – The event occurs if all of the input events occur in a specific order
- Inhibit Gate – The event occurs if the input event occurs, along with a conditional input event

Additional Problem-Solving Tools

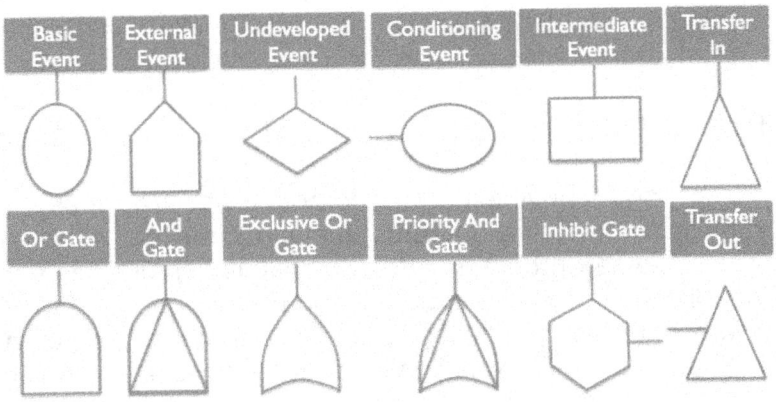

Fault Tree Analysis Process:

1. Select and clearly define the top-level failure for analysis with fault tree (one top-level failure per fault tree); inputs to a fault tree analysis may include defect records, warranty records, service logs, customer complaint logs, system performance requirements, FMEA, etc.
2. Under the top-level failure, add inputs or faults that contribute to the top-level failure
3. Under each input or fault, list all actual causes of failure; if available, list the probabilities for each cause
4. Draw the fault tree diagram (top-level failure – logic gates – inputs or faults – logic gates – actual causes) using the basic fault tree symbols and logic gates
5. Analyze the fault tree to determine actual root cause(s) of the top-level failure; using a cause-and-effect diagram and/or 5 Why root cause analysis at this step may be useful to determine root cause(s)

An example of using fault tree analysis is when an engineering team is formed to determine causes of car door airbags not deploying on a side impact. The team lists "car door airbags not deploying on side impact" as the top-level failure on a fault tree. They use design specifications, historical data, and crash test results to determine input faults to the top-level failure, along with their associated causes. The information is used to create a fault tree, analyze it for root cause of the input faults, and conduct tests to validate assumptions. The team creates a solution implementation plan to implement corrections

Additional Problem-Solving Tools

to the design in order to prevent causes of the faults and top-level failure.

FMEA to Understand Failure Modes and Effects

While the saying, "If anything can go wrong, it will." has been quoted as Murphy's Law, certainly an addendum to it could be "... and new solutions create new problems." For a new solution resulting from a problem-solving effort, Failure Modes and Effect Analysis (FMEA) is an excellent approach to employ for finding and mitigating potential causes of failures. FMEA was first introduced in the late 1940s by the US Military, adopted and modified in the early 1960s by NASA, and is now widely used in most every industry.

FMEA can be used for:

- Predicting failures or issues with new solutions
- Control points to sustain new solutions
- Root cause analysis for existing services, products, or processes

FMEA should be used when:

- The solution results in a new process or approach
- The solution impacts safety, quality, or customer service
- The solution is large, complex, and costly
- New solutions will be evaluated and implemented
- Data collection and root cause analysis will be performed

Benefits of conducting FMEA include:

- Increase focus and attention on potential failure causes
- Proactive approach for preventing the causes of potential failures from becoming failures
- Provide a consistent approach for analyzing, prioritizing, communicating, and managing potential failures
- Provide an approach to efficiently and effectively mitigate potential failures
- Provide a collaborative team environment
- Save cost and time by identifying, prioritizing, and managing potential failures

Additional Problem-Solving Tools

Failure Modes and Effects Analysis Process:

1. Assemble a cross-functional team of subject matter experts (SMEs), who will be prepared for the session upon completing prework on the FMEA topic
2. With support of the team, complete the FMEA template as described in the following steps
3. Fill in the FMEA header

VALUE	Failure Modes and Effects Analysis (FMEA)		
Item/Process:	Preparer:	Number:	
Team		Date:	

4. Fill in process steps or requirements for FMEA topic

#	Process Function (Step) (Requirements)	Potential Failure Modes (What could go wrong with process inputs, components, information, etc.)	Potential Failure Effects (The effect the failure mode has on the Output or Y variable)	S E V	Potential Causes of the Failure Mode	O C C	Current Process Controls (that could prevent or detect the Cause)	D E T	R P N
1									
2									
3									
4									
5									
6									
7									

5. List potential failure modes for each step in the process or each requirement; there may be multiple failure modes for each
6. List potential failure effects for each failure mode
7. Rank the "severity" of each potential failure mode and effect; ranking is typically 1 to 10, with 10 being the most severe

Rating	Description
10	Dangerously high
9	Extremely high
8	Very high
7	High
6	Moderate
5	Low
4	Very Low
3	Minor
2	Very Minor
1	None

8. List potential causes for each potential failure mode
9. Rank the likelihood of "occurrence" for each potential failure mode cause (1-to-10 ranking, 10 is the most likely to occur)

Additional Problem-Solving Tools

Rating	Description
10	**Very High:** Failure is almost inevitable
9	**High:** Failures occur almost as often as not
8	**High:** Repeated failures
7	**High:** Failures occur often
6	**Moderately High:** Frequent failures
5	**Moderate:** Occasional failures
4	**Moderately Low:** Infrequent failures
3	**Low:** Relatively few failures
2	**Low:** Failures are few and far between
1	**Remote:** Failure is unlikely

10. List current process controls for each of the potential failure mode causes
11. Rank current process controls for the "detection" ability of the potential cause or the failure mode after occurrence (1-to-10 ranking, 10 is the most uncertain to detect)

Rating	Description
10	Absolute Uncertainty
9	Very Remote
8	Remote
7	Very Low
6	Low
5	Moderate
4	Moderately High
3	High
2	Very High
1	Almost Certain

12. Calculate the risk priority number (RPN) by multiplying *severity x occurrence x detection* to prioritize actions; the highest (or predetermined cut-off level) RPNs are addressed, along with any company, industry, or customer requirements with high-severity ratings
13. List recommended actions for identified RPNs and high-severity ratings
14. List the responsible person and target dates for each recommended action
15. List action taken and re-rank severity, occurrence, and detection
16. Recalculate the RPN, based on actions taken
17. Repeat the FMEA process, as necessary and as part of continuous improvement cycles

Additional Problem-Solving Tools

Recommend Actions	Responsible Person & Target Date	Actions Taken	S E V	O C C	D E T	R P N

Force Field Analysis to Understand Energies

Once a solution is determined, conducting force field analysis on the solution is a powerful technique to ensure success of implementation and adoption of the solution. Kurt Lewin's 1940s Force Field Analysis is a very powerful, yet simple, tool to evaluate opposing forces (drivers and restrainers) and to determine actions for moving toward implementing a solution. The use of force field analysis has expanded over the years from its origins in social science to being used in a variety of business situations.

It is a proactive approach to understand variables and forces around a particular goal or objective, and to act on the variables in a positive manner. For example, the force field analysis supports efforts to implement and sustain problem-solving solutions.

Why do solutions get delayed or sometimes fail? One possible reason for this may be because a force field analysis was not conducted, and thus restraining forces and driving forces were not understood nor managed appropriately. Consider the next time you launch a new solution or process. Why not use a force field analysis to understand where to focus actions and efforts?

Force field analysis may be used when:

- A new solution or process is being evaluated for viability
- A new solution or process is being evaluated for implementation
- There is concern for solution sustainability

Benefits of force field analysis include:

- Proactive approach to define and mitigate restraining forces

Additional Problem-Solving Tools

- Provide input for developing a solution implementation plan and assigning resources
- Provide a collaborative team environment
- Bring together diverse backgrounds and experiences

Force Field Analysis Process:

1. Assemble a cross-functional team of subject matter experts (SMEs) who will be prepared for the session as a result of completing pre-work on the topic
2. Construct a force field analysis diagram (as follows) on a flipchart or use a template projected onto the screen
3. Validate the current situation or problem
4. List the goal or objective of the solution being implemented
5. List the driving forces, and rank forces from 1 to 5, with 5 being the strongest
6. List the restraining forces, and rank the forces from 1 to 5, with 5 being the strongest
7. Define an action plan describing "who, what, and when" to leverage or strengthen drivers, and to mitigate or eliminate restrainers
8. Execute and manage the action plan to ensure success

An example of using force field analysis is a cross-functional problem solving team who defines a solution to significantly modify a current material planning and handling process. During the step, construct the solution, the team uses a force field analysis to understand the drivers, which would be leveraged or strengthened, and the restrainers, which must be eliminated or mitigated, to be successful with implementation of the new process. The information from the force field analysis helps the team define an action plan to implement a sustainable solution.

A simple matrix tool, as noted in the following image, will be helpful for facilitating a force field analysis session as part of a problem solving effort:

Additional Problem-Solving Tools

VALUE GENERATION PARTNERS — Force Field Analysis

Facilitator:		Date:	
Goal or Solution Statement:			
List Drivers	Score	List Restrainers	Score
Total Driver Score	0	Total Restrainer Score	0

Graphical Analysis to Visualize Issues

Attributed to Fred Barnard's ad in Printer's Ink in 1921 is the now often used and cited saying, "A picture is worth a thousand words." Graphical analysis includes images and pictures, which are a powerful set of visual tools for your Problem Solving for Success efforts. Spawned from teachings of W. Edwards Deming and Kaoru Ishikawa sometime around 1950, these tools have become mainstays in a problem solving professional's toolbox.

The following are useful and powerful examples of graphical analysis tools, which can facilitate and support root cause problem solving efforts. These same graphical analysis tools may be used later in the problem solving effort to verify and sustain successful solution implementation.

Additional Problem-Solving Tools

Control Charts are graphical tools used to understand and analyze process changes and variation, over time, as depicted in the following images. Questions to consider when using controls charts are:

1. Is the process in control and stable?
2. Is the process out of control with an assignable or special cause variation?
3. Is the process out of control with systematic variation, such as trends or cycles?

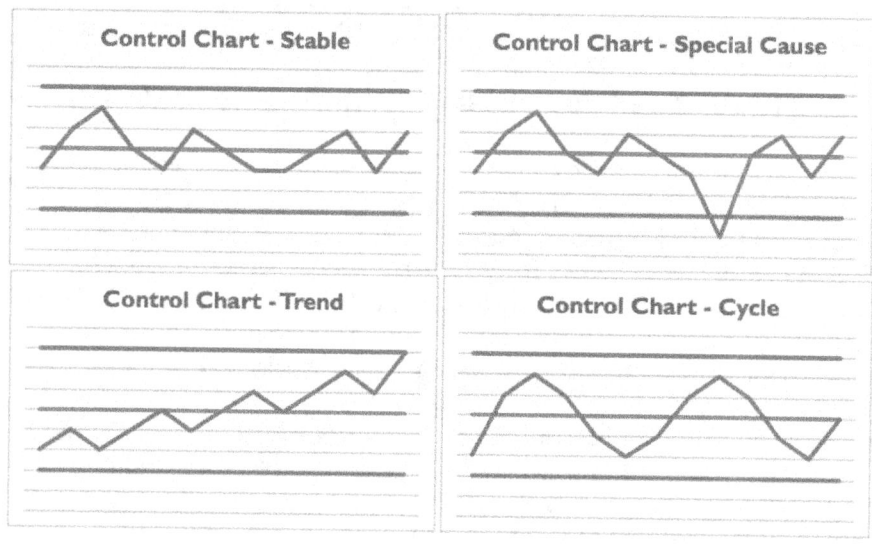

Additional Problem-Solving Tools

Histogram is a graphical tool, depicted in the following images, used to display and analyze the shape of a frequency distribution of occurrences for a variable data set. Questions to consider when using histograms are:

1. Is the distribution normal or bell shaped?
2. Is the distribution bimodal or multimodal indicating a mixture of more than one process or input?
3. Is the distribution negatively or positively skewed?

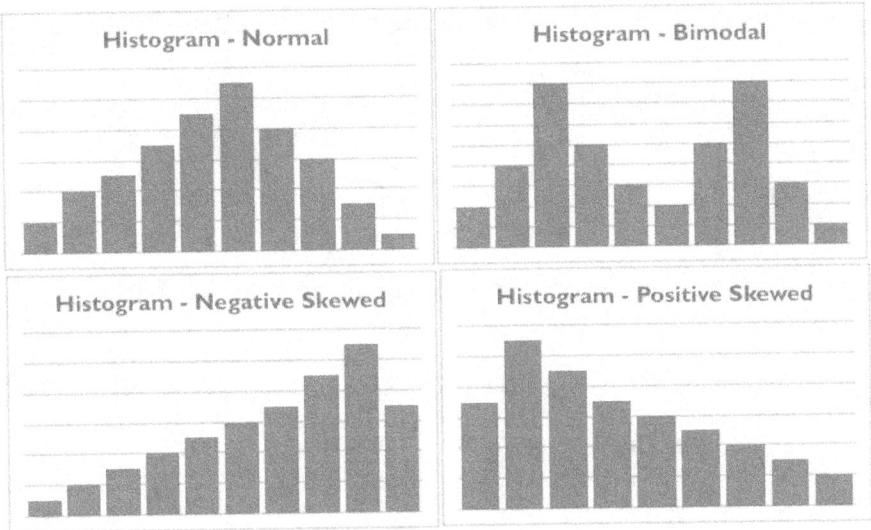

Additional Problem-Solving Tools

Pareto Chart is a graphical tool, depicted in the following images, used to identify significant categories on which to focus additional or continued efforts. Questions to consider when using Pareto charts are:

1. Are there multiple main causes, such as the top left image?
2. Is there a single main cause, such as the top right image?
3. Is there no main cause detectable, such as the bottom left image?
4. Is too much information captured in a miscellaneous category with no main cause detectable, such as the bottom right image?

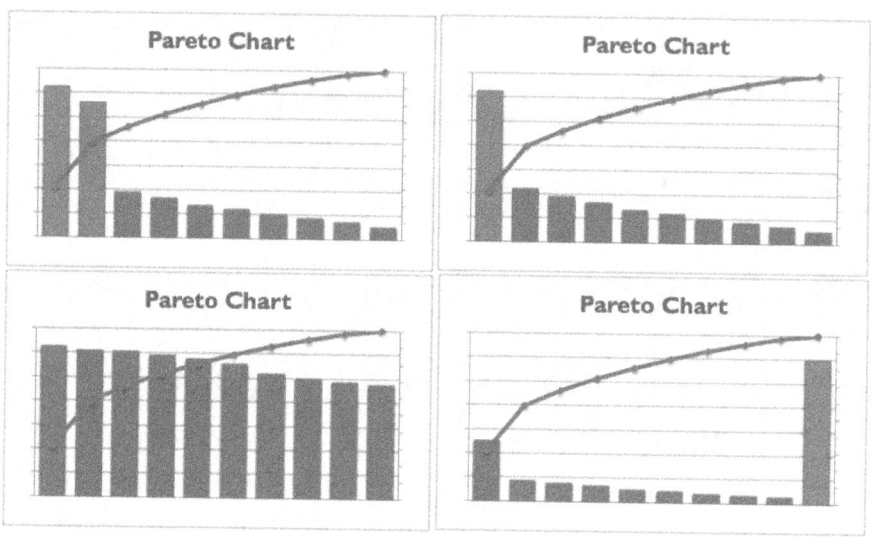

Additional Problem-Solving Tools

Scatter Diagram is a graphical tool used to compare and analyze two sets of input variable data for a correlation or relationship, as depicted in the following images. Questions to consider when using scatter diagrams are:

1. Is there a relationship or correlation between the two variables?
2. Is the relationship or correlation strong or weak?
3. Is the relationship or correlation negative or positive?

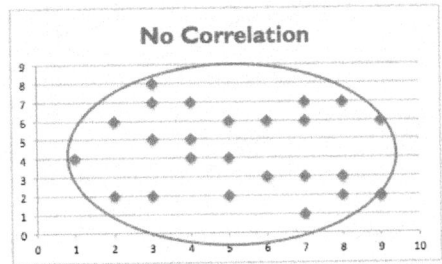

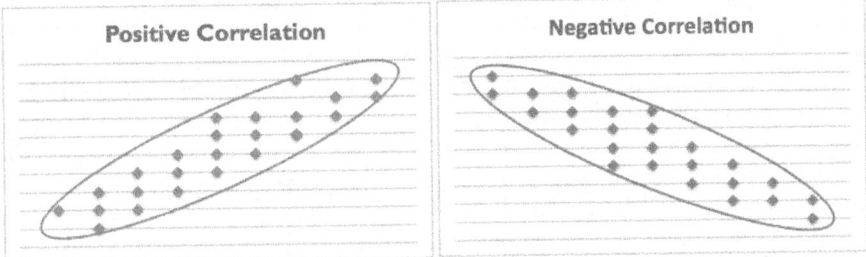

Additional Problem-Solving Tools

Stratification is a graphical tool, depicted in the following image, used to analyze separations or patterns in a data set, based on two or more input variables. Questions to consider when using stratification are:

1. Do the input variables show differences in the patterns?
2. Are the differences weak or strong?
3. Are the differences in the same or different directions?

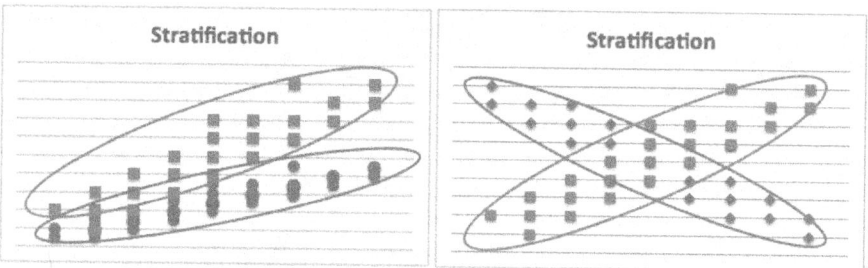

A picture really is worth a thousand words, and using these simple graphical analysis tools can be very helpful and powerful to include in root cause problem solving.

Meeting Agenda and Minutes

Paul Axtell, author of Meetings Matter, stated, "Meetings are at the heart of an effective organization, and each meeting is an opportunity to clarify issues, set new directions, sharpen focus, create alignment, and move objectives forward."

Agenda and minutes are appropriate and useful any time a group of people comes together to discuss, plan, and decide on topics and outcomes.

Benefits of using an agenda and minutes include:

- Provide a collaborative team environment
- Provide an approach to document and monitor meeting assignments
- Increase focus and attention on actions and decisions resulting from meetings
- Save time and resources by adding structure and discipline to

Additional Problem-Solving Tools

meeting management
- Provide a consistent approach for efficiently and effectively managing meeting inputs and outputs

Agenda and Minutes Process:

1. Determine the meeting logistics such as subject, objective, location, call-in number, date, chairperson, recorder, and invitees
2. Determine meeting topics, who is responsible, as well as meeting start time, duration, and desired results
3. Distribute the agenda in advance of the meeting to allow invitees to review and prepare
4. Conduct meeting based on agenda; chairperson manages the agenda; recorder documents the minutes
5. Distribute minutes within 24 hours of the meeting, describing who is responsible for certain actions, decisions made, and due dates
6. Utilize minutes for follow-up meetings and action status updates, as necessary

The following template works well for meeting agendas and minutes, as part of a problem solving effort:

VALUE GENERATION PARTNERS — Problem Solving Meeting Agenda

Meeting Subject:					
Meeting Objective:				Date:	
Location/Call-in Number:					
Chair:				Recorder:	
Invited:					
Attended:					
#	Who	Meeting Topic	Start	Duration	Comments
1		Review agenda		5 min	
2					
3					
4					
5					
6		Topics for next meeting/close		10 min	
7		Close Meeting		0 min	

Problem Solving Meeting Minutes

#	Action/Decision/Comments
1	
2	
3	
4	
5	
6	
7	

Additional Problem-Solving Tools

Mind Mapping to Generate and Analyze Ideas

Mind mapping is a powerful, simple tool to use in a brainstorming session to visually represent and analyze ideas. It is a pictorial-style thinking approach, which focuses on one central topic and allows information to be structurally portrayed for analysis and prioritization.

Unlike lists of ideas generated from typical brainstorming approaches, ideas generated through mind mapping connect to a single central topic in a branch-like diagram. Each new idea may generate an additional branch connected directly to the central topic, or expanded as a sub-idea from an existing main idea.

Mind mapping may be useful when:

- Little or no quantitative data is available
- Creative thinking and problem solving are useful
- A team approach and input are preferred
- Organizing and presenting information in a visual method are desired

Benefits of mind mapping include:

- Bring together diverse backgrounds and experiences
- Provide an approach for generating creative thoughts and ideas
- Provide an approach for pictorial presentation of ideas
- Provide a collaborative team environment

Mind Mapping Process:

1. Assemble a team of participants who were briefed and come prepared to engage in the mind mapping central topic
2. Write the central topic on a board or flip chart
3. Brainstorm, write, and connect main ideas related to the central topic on the board
4. Brainstorm, write, and connect sub-ideas related to the main ideas on the board
5. Continue to brainstorm ideas until no additions are necessary
6. Use mind map for next phase of the problem solving effort, such as an implementation plan or prioritization process

Additional Problem-Solving Tools

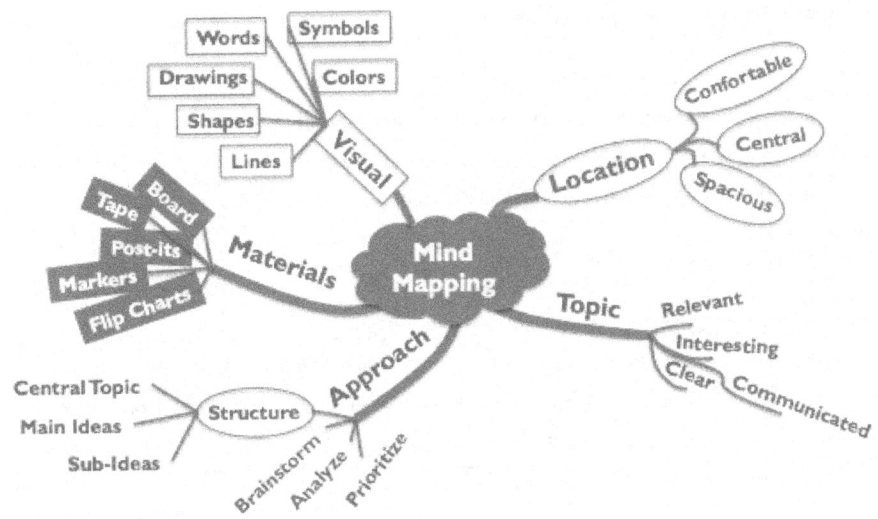

Mind mapping examples:

Central Topic Examples	Potential Main Ideas to Connect to the Central Topic
Plan a Vacation	Destinations, Timing, Length of Stay, Method of Transportation
Plan a Meeting	Location, Duration, Attendees, Agenda
Landscape Yard	Size, Location, Flowers, Shrubbery
Design a Smart Phone	Size, Features, Functionality, Colors, Materials, Manufacturer
Open a Restaurant	Location, Menu, Service Type, Seating Style

The central topics listed in the examples above will be written at the center of the mind map, and the main ideas listed become branches. Participants continue to brainstorm potential main ideas to connect to the central topic and sub-ideas to connect to the main ideas. Once the mind map is complete, participants will evaluate the ideas for relevancy, priority, and next steps.

Multivoting for Reaching Group Consensus

Multivoting is a simple, efficient approach for reaching group consensus on the most important ideas on which to focus from a list that has been generated by the group. It can be thought of as reducing the trivial many to the critical few.

Additional Problem-Solving Tools

Multivoting may be used when:

- There are too many ideas on which to focus
- Consensus for selecting ideas is preferred
- Team approach and input are preferred
- Opinions vary on which ideas should take priority

Benefits of multivoting include:

- Provide a collaborative team environment
- Provide a consistent approach for selecting ideas
- Provide an effective and efficient approach for selecting ideas
- Facilitate building consensus
- Save time and cost by focusing on select ideas

Multivoting Process:

1. Assemble a team prepared to conduct multivoting session on an existing list of ideas or by brainstorming a new list of ideas
2. Write each idea on a flip chart and assign consecutive numbers, starting with one (1) through the entire list of ideas
3. Provide each participant with a limited number of colored dot stickers (usually one-third of the total number of ideas listed)
4. Ask participants to vote on their choice for the top ideas by placing a dot next to an idea; determine the maximum number of votes each participant may post on a single idea; if appropriate, voting may be done in confidence by asking participants to write on a piece of paper their votes for top choices
5. Record the total number of votes for each idea; if necessary, repeat the multivoting process on the ideas with the highest votes until the list of ideas with the most votes is manageable for taking action
6. Develop an implementation plan (who, what, and when) for ideas with the most votes

Additional Problem-Solving Tools

A team challenged with determining select ideas, from a list of 20, on which to focus their efforts, characterizes an example of using multivoting. A list of brainstorming ideas is developed by the team to reduce customer wait time at a service desk for issuing license plates and car titles in a government office. The team decides to use multivoting to select the top five ideas from the list. Using a cut-off value of five votes after the first round of voting, there are eight ideas remaining on the list. With limited resources and time, the team wishes to reduce the list to five ideas. The team conducts a second round of multivoting on the remaining list of eight ideas; it becomes clear by the number of votes those top five ideas the team feels is most important to implement. There is full support and ownership by the team and sponsor to proceed with implementation of the ideas numbered 2, 5, 6, 10, and 17. See the voting table image for the votes cast in two rounds.

Idea No.	1st Vote Score	New List	2nd Vote Score	Final List
1	0			
2	10	2	7	2
3	0			
4	7	4	0	
5	9	5	6	5
6	6	6	5	6
7	0			
8	6	8	0	
9	0			
10	7	10	6	10
11	0			
12	4			
13	5	13	2	
14	0			
15	3			
16	0			
17	8	17	6	17
18	0			
19	3			
20	2			

Nominal Group Technique to Generate/Rank Ideas

Nominal group technique (NGT) is an effective approach to generate, clarify, and rank ideas. It is a combination of brainstorming and multivoting, with a twist on the idea-generation component of the process. It provides an approach to include all participants in the discussion process, thus avoiding concerns, conflict, and criticism.

Nominal group technique ground rules:

- No idea is a bad idea

Additional Problem-Solving Tools

- Encourage participation from all
- Do not criticize or evaluate ideas
- Solicit quantity of ideas
- No titles in the room
- Record ideas; build on those ideas

Nominal group technique may be used when:

- Strength of personalities vary within the group of participants
- Levels of authority vary within the group of participants
- There is reluctance to participate by some participants
- There are new members to the group
- Topic of the session may be perceived by some as controversial in nature
- Generating a quantity of ideas is difficult

Benefits of nominal group technique include:

- Provide an approach for equal participation
- Provide a safe, fair environment for participants
- Bring together diverse backgrounds and experiences
- Provide a collaborative team environment
- Provide an effective and efficient approach for generating, clarifying, and prioritizing ideas

Nominal Group Technique Process:

1. Assemble a cross-functional team of participants who are briefed and come prepared to engage in the brainstorming session
2. Prepare the session participants by facilitating introductions and reviewing the brainstorming topic, ground rules, expectations, concerns, deliverables of the session
3. Allow participants five to ten minutes in silence to generate ideas related to the session topic and deliverables; participants will have been briefed on and prepared for the topic prior to the session
4. In a round robin arrangement, ask each participant to verbally state one idea at a time with no discussion or evaluation; facilitator records each idea on a flip chart exactly as presented; continue presenting and recording ideas until participants have no more ideas to add to the list or the agreed-upon time limit is

Additional Problem-Solving Tools

reached
5. Review and clarify each idea on the list, seeking approval by idea contributor; reword, where necessary; with agreement by participants, strike an idea from the list
6. Prioritize the ideas using impact/effort matrix, multivoting, pairwise comparison, selection matrix, etc.
7. Use these prioritized ideas for the next phase of the problem solving effort

Pairwise Comparison to Prioritize Options

Pairwise comparison (also known as paired comparison) is a powerful and simple tool for prioritizing and ranking multiple options relative to each other. It is the process of using a matrix-style tool to compare each option in pairs and determine which is the preferred choice or has the highest level of importance based on defined criteria. At the end of the comparison process, each option has a rank or relative rating, as compared to the rest of the options.

Pairwise comparison may be useful when:

- Quantitative, objective data is not available as part of the evaluation and decision-making process
- It is necessary to determine which solutions, projects, problems, etc., to focus on when resources are limited
- A choice must be made from several options, and it is necessary to screen the options relative to each other
- Decision or selection criteria must be weighted or ranked for importance relative to each other prior to using in a decision or selection matrix

Benefits of pairwise comparison include:

- Provide a consistent and efficient approach for prioritizing or ranking multiple options
- Provide a collaborative team environment
- Reduce emotion and bias from the decision-making process

Pairwise Comparison Process:

1. Assemble a team of stakeholders who are vested in the pairwise

Additional Problem-Solving Tools

comparison options and topic
2. List the options for comparison along the "X" and "Y" axes of the Pairwise Comparison Matrix; in the image, notice that each option is assigned a letter to represent the option in the comparison matrix
3. Determine the criteria for comparison, such as which option is preferred in terms of cost, customer impact, financial impact, resource requirements, risk level, etc.
4. Compare each option in the rows to each option in the columns, and place the letter of the preferred or most important option in the cell, which aligns the two options; notice that the matrix does not allow options to be compared to themselves, or to each other more than one time
5. Once all options are compared, sum the number of times each letter appears in the matrix for the prioritization ranking of each option; note that the matrix template performs the calculation; if necessary or useful, convert the rankings to percentages
6. Use the prioritization ranking of the options for the next phase of the problem solving effort

An example of using pairwise comparison is a team working with the sponsor to prioritize seven deliverables. The team lists the deliverables from "A" to "G" on both axes of the pairwise comparison matrix. Using the matrix, each deliverable is compared in pairs. (Example: Compare deliverable A to deliverable B, then deliverable A to deliverable C, etc.)

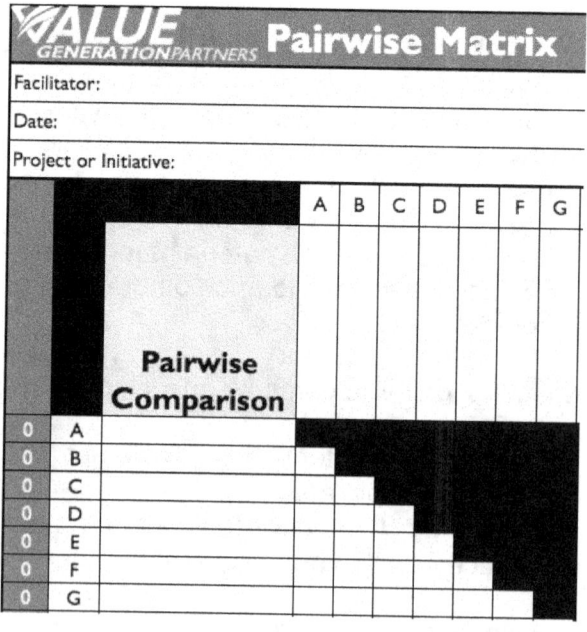

During the comparison process, the sponsor determines which is the most important deliverable in the pair, and its letter is placed in the corresponding cell. At the end of the comparison, the deliverables are ranked for priority by the number of times a deliverable's representative letter is used.

SIPOC to Summarize High-Level Process

SIPOC is a document summarizing a high-level process, including **S**uppliers, **I**nputs, **P**rocess, **O**utputs and **C**ustomers. A completed SIPOC includes a list of the suppliers to the process, inputs to the process, the process itself, outputs of the process, and a list of customers of the process. Included in the SIPOC template is an additional column, titled "CTC," or Critical-To-Customer; it contains a list of the critical-to-customer characteristics expected *from* the process *by* the customer *of* the process.

A SIPOC may be useful when:

- A process is being analyzed as part of a problem solving effort
- Team members are not familiar with the process and its elements
- Process documentation is outdated or it is necessary to define a new process
- Procedures, work instructions, and/or training materials are being developed

Benefits of a SIPOC include:

- Provide input for training materials and process documentation
- Provide a starting point for problem solving or process improvement
- Provide a consistent approach for analyzing and improving a process
- Provide a simple and high-level view of the process and its elements
- Provide a collaborative team environment

SIPOC Documentation Process:

1. Assemble a cross-functional team of subject matter experts (SMEs)
2. Draw the SIPOC diagram or project the electronic template on a screen

Additional Problem-Solving Tools

3. Define the high-level process (beginning to end) in a few steps as a vertical block diagram in the process section of the SIPOC; the order in which the columns of the SIPOC template are completed may vary depending on the team and the facilitator
4. Document the outputs from the process including materials, services, and information
5. Document the internal and external customers that receive the outputs of the process (customers may also be suppliers)
6. Document the inputs to the process including materials, services, and information
7. Document the internal and external suppliers of the inputs to the process (suppliers may also be customers)
8. Added to the traditional SIPOC, you may wish to document the critical-to-customer (CTC) characteristics expected from the process; the CTCs must be verified with customers of the process

A SIPOC may be used as an input to documenting and improving processes. It is a powerful tool for identifying and documenting the complete list of process elements. The following template works well for creating a SIPOC, as part of a problem solving effort:

VALUE GENERATION PARTNERS — SIPOC

Problem Solver:					Date:	
Suppliers	Inputs	Process	Outputs	Customers	CTCs	

Solution Selection Matrix for Prioritizing Ideas

A solution selection matrix is a powerful selection tool used to choose between multiple solution alternatives during a problem-solving effort. Solution selection matrix may be used in combination with other decision-making tools, such as decision tree analysis and impact/effort analysis.

A solution selection matrix may be used when:

Additional Problem-Solving Tools

- The current process has problems, issues, errors, or defects
- The current process, product, or service requires improvement
- Choosing the best solution among several potential solutions
- The current solution is not meeting customer requirements or performing as required

Benefits of a solution selection matrix include:

- Reduce emotion and bias from the decision-making process
- Provide a consistent approach for selecting the best solution among several options
- Save cost and time by efficiently and effectively selecting the best solution
- Provide a collaborative team environment

Solution Selection Matrix Process:

1. Assemble a cross-functional team of subject matter experts who will be prepared for the solution selection session with pre-work on the topic
2. Draw a solution selection matrix on a board or flipchart, or project an electronic matrix on a screen
3. List or brainstorm potential solutions to eliminate the current problems or issues
4. List or brainstorm selection criteria to evaluate potential solutions; the selection criteria may be determined with input from the problem-solving sponsor or process owner
5. Determine a weight factor for each of the selection criteria; weights may be determined using pairwise comparison or simply ranking on a scale of 1 to 5
6. Evaluate each potential solution against the criteria, and enter a rank of 1 if the solution "does not meet" the criteria, 5 for "somewhat meets" the criteria, or 9 for "fully meets" the criteria
7. Determine the weighted score by multiplying each selection criteria weight by the individual solution score, then summing the total for each concept; note that the matrix template performs these calculations
8. Determine which solution(s) to implement in order to eliminate issues and problems with the current solution or process

Additional Problem-Solving Tools

An example using a solution selection matrix is a continuous improvement team analyzing several potential solutions to reduce defects found during testing at a software development company. The team analyzes the process and the causes of the defects, and then develops a list of eight potential solutions to prevent the defects. The potential solutions are evaluated against the selection criteria listed in the matrix; those potential solutions with the highest scores are selected for implementation.

The following template works well for conducting solution selection, as part of a problem solving effort:

VALUE GENERATIONPARTNERS			**Solution-Selection Matrix**									
Problem Solver:									Date:			
SMART Goal:												
				Selection Criteria								
				Low Effort	High Impact	Acceptable Cost	Acceptable Time	Acceptable Risk	Resources Available	Cultural Acceptance	Addresses Root Cause		
			Weight									Total Score	Implement (Y or N)
Output (y) or CTC	Root Cause (x)	Potential Solution	(1=No, 5=Somewhat, 9=Yes)										
												0	
												0	
												0	
												0	
												0	
												0	
												0	

Status Reporting for Updating Stakeholders

Status reporting and feedback are fundamental to the successful execution and governance of problem solving. Status reports are conducted on a weekly or bi-weekly cycle, depending on the size, complexity, duration of problem solving, and depending on stakeholder needs.

A status report is used when:

- Problem solving impacts external customers

Additional Problem-Solving Tools

- Problem solving is important to the organization's strategies and success
- Sponsor, stakeholders, and senior leaders are heavily engaged and interested in problem solving

Benefits of a status report include:

- Provide an informative and collaborative team environment
- Save cost and time through accountability, visibility, and feedback loop
- Provide a consistent, efficient, and effective approach for reporting problem-solving status, health, accomplishments, issues, and risks
- Increase focus and attention on problem-solving governance and accountability by key stakeholders and problem-solving team

Status Reporting Cycle:

1. Prepare and update the status report with current problem-solving information: Brief overview of problem solving; activities and actions planned for the next reporting cycle; accomplishments since the last reporting cycle; metrics for measuring problem-solving health and success; issues and risks, along with plans for resolution
2. Schedule and conduct status report update with sponsor, team, and key stakeholders
3. Gather feedback on problem-solving status and health
4. Incorporate feedback into problem-solving plan and schedule

It is fundamental for larger and more complex problem-solving efforts to include a status report as part of the review process. The following template works well for conducting problem-solving status reporting, supplementing the A3 Problem Solving for Success Worksheet.

Additional Problem-Solving Tools

Problem Solving Status Report

Problem Overview		Metrics	Status
Date:			Not Started
Problem Solver:			Not Started
Sponsor:			Not Started
Deliverables:			Not Started
Goal:		**Problem Accomplishments**	
Scope:			
Metrics:			
Other:			

Problem Next Steps	Due	Status	Issues/Risks and Resolutions	Status
		Not Started		
		Not Started		Not Started
		Not Started		Not Started
		Not Started		Not Started
		Not Started		Not Started

Training Plan for Sustaining Solutions

Most solutions result in a new method or process, which will likely require some amount and level of training. In today's fast-paced environment, it is difficult to find time to conduct training sessions, so the necessary training may be delivered in one or more methods.

- **eLearning** – participants take the training via computer at their own pace
- **Instructor-led** – participants attend an in-class session that is facilitated by an instructor
- **Virtual** – participants dial-in and log-on to a web-based training session that is led by a remote instructor
- **Blended learning** – participants may take the training in a combination of instructor-led, virtual, and/or eLearning sessions

A training plan is useful when:

- A solution results in a new process or approach
- A solution crosses many functions or departments
- The solution impacts safety, quality, or customer service

Benefits of developing a training plan include:

Additional Problem-Solving Tools

- Provide a consistent approach for analyzing, developing, delivering, and validating training
- Provide an approach for efficiently and effectively training
- Provide a collaborative team environment
- Save cost and time by developing and delivering training appropriate to the solution

Training Plan Process:

1. Training topic is identified as part of the solution implementation or solution sustainment plan
2. A training needs analysis and materials design/development owners are identified and assigned
3. Trainer is identified and assigned
4. Training logistics – including participants, delivery date, training duration, and delivery method – are determined and defined
5. Training is delivered, evaluated, and adjusted
6. Training results are validated to ensure intent of training was achieved

The following template works well to manage a training plan when required as part of a problem-solving effort, supplementing the A3 Problem Solving for Success Worksheet.

VALUE GENERATION PARTNERS — Training Plan

Problem Solver: Date:

Analyze - Design - Develop				Deliver - Evaluate - Adjust - Validate				
Who	What	When	Other	Who		When	How	Other
Owner	Topic	Due Date	Status Comments	Trainer	Participant(s)	Date	Duration	Method	Results Comments

Summary: Problem Solving for Success

Former Secretary of State, John Foster Dulles, is credited with the quote, "The measure of success is not whether you have a tough problem to deal with, but whether it is the same problem you had last year." Problems, also known as opportunities, issues, failures, defects, etc., come in many shapes and sizes and exist in every business and industry with varying levels of impact and complexity.

This simple seven-step, fact-based approach, called Problem Solving for Success, may be applied to any problem in any industry – healthcare, construction, manufacturing, service, hospitality, non-profit, government, financial, etc.

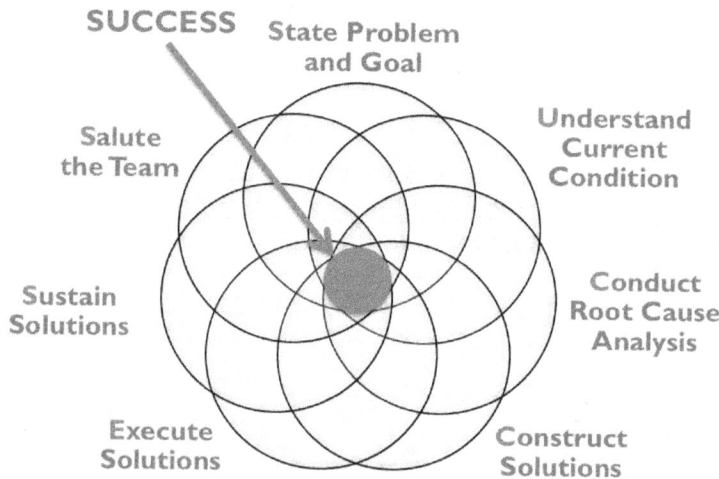

The A3 Problem Solving for Success Worksheet, found in the *Problem Solving for Success Toolbox*, is used to guide problem-solving efforts. It is a variation of an A3 Thinking PDCA template, and it is used to document, summarize, and report problem-solving progress and status.

This guide to Problem Solving for Success is designed for problem solvers of all levels, regardless of their role, business, and industry. It

Summary: Problem Solving for Success

combines the best elements of some of the simplest to most complex problem-solving approaches and methodologies into the following seven steps:

1. **State Problem and Goal** – initiate the A3 Problem Solving for Success Worksheet, document the theme of the problem, define the problem, and create a SMART goal
2. **Understand Current Condition** – document the current-state process flow
3. **Conduct Root Cause Analysis** – create a cause-and-effect diagram, list issues with the current state, analyze data, and conduct 5 Why
4. **Construct Solutions** – list potential solutions, analyze for impact and effort, pilot test and verify solutions, and define the future-state process flow
5. **Execute Solutions** – define and execute a solution implementation plan
6. **Sustain Solutions** – define and execute a solution sustainment plan, conduct sign-off, and close problem solving
7. **Salute the Team** – recognize the team; celebrate success

Employing the seven-step process of Problem Solving for Success will result in a solution that solves the problem and sustains the results.

Useful and powerful approaches to support and supplement Problem Solving for Success are further defined in **Project Management Handbook** and **Workshop Facilitation Handbook**, and are summarized in the following seven-step processes.

Project Management for Success Process:

Step One: Set-up the Project
Step Two: Understand the Requirements
Step Three: Create the Team
Step Four: Construct the Plan
Step Five: Execute the Plan
Step Six: Sign-off and Close the Project
Step Seven: Salute the Team

Workshop Facilitation for Success Process:

Summary: Problem Solving for Success

Step One: Set-up the Workshop Charter
Step Two: Understand the Logistics
Step Three: Create the Team
Step Four: Clarify the Roles and Responsibilities
Step Five: Execute the Workshop
Step Six: Share Status of Workshop
Step Seven: Salute the Team

Key to Problem Solving for Success is timely, concise, and appropriate communication. George Bernard Shaw was quoted as saying, "The single biggest problem in communication is the illusion that it has taken place." As you execute the seven-step problem-solving approach, you must ensure that in each step careful consideration is given to the impact on the many and various stakeholders, and how that impact is communicated.

Benefits of timely and concise communication include:

- Facilitates securing support for the problem-solving effort
- Clarification of roles and responsibilities
- Status of the problem-solving effort
- Updates on issues, risks, and changes
- Updates on activities, implementation plans, and training plans

We wish you much success in your pursuit of Problem Solving for Success, thereby generating greater organizational value!